When things break down or don't go as planned, there are always three archetypal questions we are called to ask ourselves: What needs to be repaired? What needs to be reimagined? And what needs to be left dismantled?

## PRAISE FOR MARK NEPO

"Lyrical, insightful, and wise, *Surviving Storms* is the guide to resilience that we find ourselves so desperately needing, both for individuals and communities. Mark Nepo's words are a potent antidote to discouragement and a heartfelt call to perseverance."     —Arianna Huffington, founder & CEO, Thrive

"Mark Nepo is our bard of the enlightened heart, a voice of tenderness, wisdom, and sanity at a time when we are in upheaval. This book will steady you as you go and help you reach your true destination."

—Mark Matousek, author of *Ethical Wisdom: The Search for a Moral Life* and *Sex Death Enlightenment: A True Story*

"Through twenty beautiful books of prose and poetry, Mark Nepo has shown us that life is a bottomless well of meaning when plumbed with the poetic imagination that is his hallmark. Now he's done it again with his insightful and empowering reflections on finding the strength to meet adversity. We need this book as we grieve our losses from climate change, a worldwide pandemic, war and threats of war, and radical inequality. Mark looks straight into the challenges we face, and still finds hope in our shared journey. The key, he says, is 'staying devoted to the difficult and beautiful journey of being human.' That's exactly what he does in this superb exploration. Count me among the deeply grateful."

—Parker J. Palmer, author of *On the Brink of Everything, Let Your Life Speak, A Hidden Wholeness*, and *The Courage to Teach*

"How can we walk through the fractured landscape of today and keep our eyes clear and our hearts open? Through his ability to find the wisdom in ordinary things, Mark Nepo shows how heartwork can deepen us on this journey, helping us to repair ourselves and the world. Here are resources for the traveler, helping us to say yes to life, awakening us to the grace that is always present."     —Llewellyn Vaughan-Lee, Ph.D., Sufi teacher and author of *Sufism: The Transformation of the Heart*

"Mark Nepo has long been a steady guide in living with an open heart. In his latest book, Mark brings a lifetime of experience and learning to bear on how we can find the strength to survive the storms life puts in our path. This book is an enduring resource for our times. Journey here and discover your own strength."     —Chip Conley, *New York Times* bestselling author and founder of the Modern Elder Academy

"Very few modern writers impress me as much as Mark Nepo with his insight, inspiration, and turns of phrase."

—Christopher Buck, publisher of *OMTimes*

"Mark Nepo is an exceptional writer and an amazing teacher and spiritual guide."

—Paul Grondahl, director of
the New York State Writers Institute

"There's a reason the heart is located at the center of every sentient being. It is within our heart-center, our core, that we find our connection to and feel our coherence with the Divine. And it is through the wisdom and power of the heart that we discover the innate love, courage, and strength to transcend any challenge, regardless of what is happening in our lives and the world. *Surviving Storms* is your fail-safe guide to that discovery and exploration, one that ultimately leads to your freedom and empowerment."

—Michael Bernard Beckwith, founder & CEO of
Agape International Spiritual Center and
author of *Life Visioning* and *Spiritual Liberation*

"In this luminous collection of reflections on the turbulence of our times, my friend Mark Nepo once again beckons us toward the beauty in the brokenness, the holiness in the hot mess, and the call to oneness at the heart of our sense of disconnection. In reclaiming our kinship with all life, this book helps us increase our capacity to participate in mending and rebuilding the world."

—Mirabai Starr, author of
*Caravan of No Despair* and *Wild Mercy*

"There are those times—so widespread right now—when storms of conflict, confusion, and adversity rage within and all around us. Who doesn't yearn for the wisdom and ways to endure, and perhaps to even grow through it all? In *Surviving Storms*, spiritual teacher, poet, and cancer survivor Mark Nepo blesses us with a spark in the dark . . . soul-stirring inspiration to reconnect us with the deepest things in life. Let this book help you, as it did me, become undeniably and passionately rooted in the courage, resilience, and greatness of the awakened heart."

—Dr. Roger Teel, spiritual leader and
author of *This Life is Joy*

surviving
storms

## ALSO BY MARK NEPO

# surviving storms

## finding the strength to meet adversity

# MARK NEPO

ST. MARTIN'S
ESSENTIALS
NEW YORK

First published in the United States by St. Martin's Essentials, an imprint of St. Martin's Publishing Group

www.stmartins.com

Designed by Kelly S. Too

The Library of Congress Cataloging-in-Publication Data is available upon request.

ISBN 978-1-250-86215-0 (hardcover)
ISBN 978-1-250-86214-3 (ebook)

Our books may be purchased in bulk for promotional, educational, or business use. Please contact your local bookseller or the Macmillan Corporate and Premium Sales Department at 1-800-221-7945, extension 5442, or by email at MacmillanSpecialMarkets@macmillan.com.

First Edition: 2022

10  9  8  7  6  5  4  3  2  1

For all the great teachers of heart I have met along the way, the first being Grandma Minnie, whose immigrant heart plowed its way like a whale across the ocean and the century so that her son could become a woodworker and her grandson a poet.

# CONTENTS

The old world is gone and still,
one candle can light many, if we
work with what we're given and
resist the suffering in not suffering.

—MN


Know that every deed counts, that every word
is power. . . . Above all, remember that you must
build your life as if it were a work of art.

—Abraham Heschel

# The Remaking of Humanity

WE LIVE IN a turbulent time. Storms are everywhere, of every shape and size. And like every generation before us, like every soul's journey on Earth, we must learn the art of surviving storms, so we can endure and build a better world.

The reason heartwork is so important in surviving storms is that, as a tree needs to deepen its roots and widen its trunk to endure the force of unexpected storms, we need to know our true self so we can deepen our roots and solidify our connection to all Spirit and all life. Then, we, too, can endure the force of unexpected storms. This is especially relevant now.

Every generation has its share of turbulence and chaos—personal storms, relational storms, life storms. And all the traditions offer practices and resources to help us be strong enough and kind enough to meet the challenges of our day. It is our turn to rediscover these practices and resources in order to repair ourselves and our world. All this is inner practice. All this is heartwork.

The first two chapters of this book describe the storms of our time—where we are and how we got here. They outline the fault lines of our refracted society, including: our loss of relationship, the isolation of technology, the dissolution of reality, the loss of a common good, the press of narcissism over inclusion, and our addiction to violence. The third chapter explores the nature and life of storms. And the fourth chapter unpacks the purpose of goodness.

The rest of the book describes the perennial practices and resources that we can reacquaint ourselves with in order to restore our basic human nature and transcend our perceived differences. This task is nothing short of the remaking of humanity, yet one more time.

The heart's process of renewal and connection is the oldest and most reliable resource we have. Following the heart as our teacher leads to an inner exploration we each must map for ourselves, though there are common passages along the way. Once the rubble clears, we, like those before us, are inevitably called to build the world one more time, admitting that we need each other.

As in my other books, I offer writing and conversation prompts (Questions to Walk With) for you to personalize the themes uncovered along the way. And as with my other books, I encourage you to take your time in moving through the topics opened here, so you can integrate what arises inwardly with the unfolding of your days.

Having journeyed this far, I firmly believe that by staying devoted to the difficult and beautiful journey of being human, our soul can blossom like an orchid in the dark, and we can restore our kinship with each other and all living things. The web of life is stronger than our blindness to it.

In Tony Kushner's epic play *Angels in America,* a deep refrain occurs when the main character, Prior, says repeatedly with increasing urgency and conviction that he wants more life. In his notes, Kushner reveals that what stirred this motif was his discovery that the Hebrew word for *blessing* means "more life." This is the blessing that comes from being educated by the heart—we are given more life. This is the blessing I wish for everyone who reads this book—that as a fish grows stronger for having a healthy and muscular gill, you are given more life for having an expansive and well-tuned heart.

part 1

# Where We Are

∞

Challenges are gifts that force us to
search for a new center of gravity.
Don't fight them.
Just find a new way to stand.

*—Oprah Winfrey*

# Mapping the Fault Lines

————

All serious daring starts within.

—Eudora Welty

THE LONG SWELLS of history crest and crash, century after century. The kindness and cruelty of an age expand and contract. The openness and narrowness of how we learn either grows or collapses depending on how each generation reacts to the storms they encounter and create. As I write this, a good part of humanity is in such a collapse of narrowness, in such a contraction of cruelty. And though we have crashed, the harsh beauty of waves is that they always reform, gathering all they've been through to rise and crest again. Likewise, we can learn from what we've been through. We can expand again and open our minds and hearts. We can find our way back to kindness, if we dare to see each other in ourselves and accept the truth of what we've broken. Then, we can see what needs repair. The chapters in this opening section explore where we are, how the old world is gone, as well as mapping the fault lines in our society. Then, there is the unfolding of the nature and life of storms, through which we can inhabit our place in the unending purpose of goodness.

# The Old World Is Gone

As THE PANDEMIC spread around the world, it brought moments from my cancer journey sharply before me. One profound moment in particular echoes where we are in a compelling way. It was the moment of my diagnosis more than thirty years ago. I was sitting in a doctor's office when I heard the words, "You have cancer."

I was, of course, frightened and disoriented. I thought, he must have made a mistake. How could this be me? Stunned, I left that appointment reeling. But the door I had walked through to keep that appointment was gone. There was no way back to my life before that moment. Life would never be the same. The old world was gone.

I think this transformative moment has gripped the world. Collectively, the world before the pandemic is gone. There is no way back to life before the coronavirus. We have no choice but to accept the truth of what is and love our way forward, discovering the new life unlived ahead of us.

To be sure, there is nothing glorious or mysterious about disease. The cancer I had was not as important as what it opened in me. Likewise, there is nothing glorious or mysterious about the coronavirus. It can never be as important as what it is opening in humanity. As cancer was a catalyst for transformation when I was ill, we need to ask: What is the appearance of this pandemic trying to open in us and teach us? How is it transforming us as a global family?

In the Jewish tradition, the word *sabbath* literally means "the one day we don't turn one thing into another." And we are being forced to stop, to be still, to halt our out-of-balance doing. In essence, all of humanity has been ushered into a global sabbath. We have no choice but to stop running from here to there, to stop planning, scheming, manipulating, even to stop dreaming, to stop turning one thing into another. All to be where we are, so we might discover, yet again, that everything is sacred and that we are each other.

There is an ancient Hindu ethic carried in the phrase "Thou art that." It means that, no matter our journey, no matter what befalls us, we are each other and what happens to one happens to all. And so, it is our turn to stop and behold each other, to stop and accept that we are all connected and have always been so. Despite our fears, we are being forced to accept and inhabit that taking care of ourselves is taking care of each other.

The old world is gone. The world as we have known it has broken down. And this engenders loss. No matter how we move forward, we have to grieve what is no more. This brings to mind the work of Elisabeth Kübler-Ross, the mother of the modern hospice movement. Based on her work with those who were dying, the Swiss-born psychiatrist gave voice to what she called the five stages of grief. First introduced in her book *On Death and Dying* (1969), she later confirmed that these stages are not necessarily sequential, but more a constellation of passages that we can move through, or get stuck in, in any order.

The five stages of grief are: denial, anger, bargaining, depression, and acceptance. It is clear that in pandemic America, there are substantial sections of our society that are stuck in different stages of grief now that life as we have known it has forever changed.

The part of our population stuck in denial won't accept that the virus is with us. They insist it is a hoax. They don't want the truth to be true. And part of our society is stuck in anger. They refuse to wear masks. They want to rebel and fight against someone or something because the world that we've known has been taken from us. But what are they protesting exactly—biology? And there are those who are experiencing the loss of loved ones, jobs, and life savings. They are deeply in pain, depressed at how so much is being taken away through no fault of their own. Yet, for all our pain, fear, denial, and anger, only by walking this difficult time together will we experience some form of acceptance that will allow us to make it through the storm and inhabit the future.

Since the landmark work of Kübler-Ross, our understanding of grief has evolved to include more ambiguous losses such as: loss of place, loss of time, loss of opportunity, and loss from being disenfranchised—all of which are affecting us now.

One inescapable and humbling challenge of loss is that grief requires us to make new maps. For when we lose something dear—a person or a way of life—the geography as we have known it has changed. And so, our old maps, no matter how dear, are no longer accurate, no longer of use. We have to make new maps for how to move forward. In its paradoxical way, grief forces us back into the world where we have to keep learning.

While we yearn to move on after trauma or loss, an integration of what we live through is necessary. At the same time, there is no going back to how things were before the trauma or loss. As I said, it's been more than thirty years since I almost died from cancer. While I am not preoccupied with cancer, I have never "gotten over" this experience. More deeply, I've learned that the impact of such life-changing events changes the ground we walk on. And so, I've come to accept that life rearranges us, calling us to the art of creating new maps. In deep and lasting ways, living with an open heart is how the soul maps what is.

I want to speak more personally about grief. There is an irrepressible challenge and joy in letting all things be true, not swinging from one pole of human experience to the other but letting the heart absorb and integrate everything until it releases a deeper logic of the Spirit. One of my deepest lessons in this was in a moment of grief after my father had died, the same season that our beloved dog, Mira, had died. It was a beautiful day and my heart was exhausted open, unable to choose between beauty and grief. That's when the teacher arrived, which I listened to and wrote down in this poem:

**Adrift**

Everything is beautiful and I am so sad.
This is how the heart makes a duet of
wonder and grief. The light spraying
through the lace of the fern is as delicate
as the fibers of memory forming their web
around the knot in my throat. The breeze
makes the birds move from branch to branch
as this ache makes me look for those I've lost
in the next room, in the next song, in the laugh
of the next stranger. In the very center, under
it all, what we have that no one can take
away and all that we've lost face each other.
It is there that I'm adrift, feeling punctured
by a holiness that exists inside everything.
I am so sad and everything is beautiful.

Love and loss are inextricably linked, humbling and transforming, though we would rather have our loved one back. And no matter how much we resist rejoining life, the unseen teachers move through us, rearranging the chasm we are trying to climb out of as we feel ourselves being pulled between the plethora of life and the godforsaken emptiness. Out of unbearable grief, the heart like a phoenix mysteriously emerges in time from its own ash, one heart-giving at a time.

Just the other day, Sandy Levine, the program director for the New York Open Center, died. She was a warm, gentle soul, always welcoming, always present. Sandy was why I first spoke at the Open Center, and it led to a friendship over the years. She had a way of holding space, quietly and tenderly, that softened the room before anyone entered. And without ever knowing, those who gather at the

Open Center—next month, next year—will feel closer to the truth of what matters for her lingering presence. I already miss her. She is like a flower that leaves its fragrance long after its petals fall. There is a chickadee at the feeder this morning, and as I write this, it tilts its head, much like Sandy did. And so, it begins, seeing those we love everywhere.

In facing our grief, we are asked to let so many profound things merge in our heart until the potion of life in all its mystery cleanses us and rearranges us, almost without our knowing. Then, everything is the same but different, alive again. Humanity is in this process now.

Still, there is no getting away from loss—not personally or collectively. In time, things that matter break or die or drift out of reach. The tree I prayed against was struck by lightning. The quiet friend I confided in has moved away. The old woman who would assure me of my voice has died at ninety. And the old world, for all its treasures and misfortunes, is gone. We have no choice, but to feel our grief, and to listen and hold each other through the loss in order to renew our agreement with all that matters. So we can go on.

> *In deep and lasting ways, living with an*
> *open heart is how the soul maps what is.*

## Questions to Walk With

- In your journal, identify and personalize one of Kübler-Ross's stages of grief that has been working you during this difficult time—either denial, anger, bargaining, depression, or acceptance. What are you grieving? What are you being asked to accept?
- In conversation with a friend or loved one, describe a time you turned one thing into another when it needed to be left alone. How did your interference with life affect you and those around you?

# Our Refracted Society

IN ORDER TO repair, we need to understand where we are broken. In order to be whole, we need to know how we are partial and limited. In order to be well, we have to diagnose where we are ill. And so, we have to admit: there is a madness afoot, eating our society from the inside out. Its symptoms include a festering disdain for knowledge and a paranoia about anything unfamiliar. Whatever kernel of reality is closest to the self-contained individual or clan is deified and worshipped until all other belief systems are seen as the enemy. Worse yet, there is a metastasis of mistrust that feels the need to tear down everything. If we are to repair and, again, be a society committed to a kinship of common human values, we need to understand how we devolved into this dispersed and self-destructive state. Just how did we get here?

Here are a few ways to describe the expanse of this social entropy. When a bridge endures internal stress fractures, no one notices until several of them connect and then, the bridge collapses. The bridge of human decency has begun to collapse in America. Consider, as well, that in pottery, when a plate starts to show a network of cracks, it's known as crazing. This is caused by a mismatch between the clay body and the glaze, which creates stresses greater than the glaze is able to withstand. If the mismatch between what's inside and outside is great enough, the plate will break. Our society has been in a process of craze and collapse. We are experiencing stresses greater than the agreements of society can currently withstand and our social contracts are starting to break.

The truth is that we are in the quaking convergence of fault lines that have been crazing our society since the industrial revolution began in England (over 260 years ago) and since the first slaves were brought to America by force (403 years ago). We need to understand these fractures in our way of life, so we can reaffirm and strengthen our social contracts.

## The Loss of Relationship

While the industrial revolution (1760–1840) was a beacon of progress around the world, one of its great costs has been the deep cuts it made in the life of our relationships and we have been compensating for this loss ever since. The introduction of places of work outside the farm and, eventually, outside the local community disrupted the bonds of home. The introduction of the assembly line and the specialization of labor further disrupted the life of relationship at work itself. And the growing obsession with profit at all cost began to dehumanize the worker.

One of the great thinkers to foresee all this was Karl Marx (1818–1883). Before we go further, it's important to note that, because of the brutal failure of communism, the mention of Marx is often shunned. However, the German philosopher offered important insights into the nature of society.

As early as 1844, Marx told us that an estranged and divided society breeds an estranged and divided citizen. He proposed that an *alien nation,* one that doesn't value relationship, gives rise to personal *alienation.* In fact, Marx coined the term and thought of *alienists* as therapists who would tend to the repair of the estranged and alienated individual, bringing them back in accord with their basic human nature.

We are suffering great alienation today, as thousands of our citizens are separated from aspects of their human nature, including a true sense of self and a deep regard for others. After more than two hundred years of progress, it is clear that the depth of our alienation is a systematic result of people being treated like parts in a mechanized society. These estrangements remain severe impediments to the re-emergence of compassionate communities.

Émile Durkheim (1858–1917), a French sociologist, further articulated the concept of alienation (*anomie*) when he observed that values regarding how people should treat each other were breaking down. With less attention focused on relationships, people didn't know what to expect from one another. Durkheim foresaw that as societies become more complex, people are no longer tied to one another and social bonds become impersonal. He foresaw that periods of drastic social disruption, like now, bring about greater alienation and higher rates of crime, suicide, and isolation. He described alienation as a type of social suicide associated with the loss of a more relational way of life.

The age we live in and its technological marvels have complicated the ways we are separated from life and each other, making the need to repair and reanimate our human nature more important than ever.

## The Isolation of Technology

Another obvious point of crazing in our culture is the growing isolation of technology. Not only does the life of devices separate us from actual contact with each other, but it also keeps us from experiencing the rewards of true solitude. The experiential cocoon of technology keeps us in a digital netherworld, not truly with each other and not truly alone. This is an agitated and enervating state.

Studies have shown that our over-reliance on technology prevents us from developing and deepening skills of self-reflection, dialogue, and conflict resolution. In short, our life as technology users makes our responses to the diversity of human experience extreme.

We tend to comply and obey or rebel, often in a violent way, because our ability to learn from diversity, ambiguity, and paradox remains undeveloped.

This is not to diminish the many gifts of technology. But like the industrial revolution, the technological revolution has exacted a relational and introspective cost from all of us. For lack of true relationship and true solitude makes a purgatory of our failed reach as social beings. We float, neither here nor there, neither connected to each other nor connected to ourselves. And so, our sense of the larger weave and knit of life suffers.

Since the first modern computer was delivered to the US government in 1950 (the UNIVAC 1101), our loneliness and sense of alienation has only been deepened in the last seventy years, while our search for something real and lasting has only been exacerbated. Situated further from direct experience, our loss of introspection has only diminished our capacity for acceptance—of life, of hardship, of difference, of each other, of ourselves.

Without an ability to look honestly at ourselves or to embrace a larger context of life, we fall sharply into feeling victimized and all our grievances are projected on others—our families, our co-workers, our government, the times. The pervasive sense of national isolationism has now insinuated itself into a severe and almost unreachable personal isolationism.

If we are to surface from this technological netherworld, we must find a way to restore our direct experience of life and each other. This is perennially at the heart of all compassion.

## The Dissolution of Reality

Over the last fifty-five years, we have suffered the slow dissolution of reality. First, there was the portrayal of what is not real as real, in which entertainment served as an escape from reality. This evolved over decades into a confusion about what is real and what is not. And now, Trumpism has unleashed the deliberate effort to supplant what is real with what is false, empowering a conscious effort to break from reality.

It helps here to trace two fault lines that have been prying apart our sense of social reality. The first is the infiltration of reality TV into our consciousness. The earliest reality TV shows were *The American Sportsman* (1965), *Cops* (1989), *The Real World* (1992), *Cheaters* (2000), and *Survivor* (2000).

Reality shows, which have little to do with reality, serve as a collective tranquilizer. Under the guise of being participatory, one form of reality TV seduces isolated viewers into thinking that they have actually taken an action in a community by voting for contestants. Yet after extending themselves, viewers are still isolated and longing for connection. All the while, the shows reinforce self-interest, often motivated by scarcity and fear. And viewers fantasize about being on the shows and winning, rather than facing the lives that are truly theirs to live.

Shows like *The Apprentice, Survivor,* and *Fear Factor,* to name a few, define success as the ability to outwit, outperform, out-stomach, and out-bully others in order to secure money and celebrity. In *The Apprentice,* success is determined by appeasing a patriarchal authority at all costs. *Survivor* is a romanticized training ground for the winner-take-all mentality that informs the most ruthless kind of competition. There, the voting among rivals for who stays on the show is a test of duplicity and betrayal. *Fear Factor* titillates viewers with a vicarious glimpse of people mustering the nerve to perform terrifying acts, all for the sake of winning. These contrived situations replace the miracle of finding the extraordinary in the ordinary with the need to devise more and more jarring acts until the perverse defines what is extraordinary. This, in turn, is the source of shock—not the source of wonder.

These situations are all subliminal forms of avoiding life. Paradoxically, the reality show ethos—where we gather and wait for something to save us or free us—has subverted the gifts needed to participate in actual reality. The generic reality show is voyeuristic, giving us a vicarious taste of the journey without taking the risk to enter our own life and embark on our own journey.

These shows tell young people that through self-interest and cutthroat behavior they can stay on the show and, by doing anything to anyone or even to themselves, they can please their peers and the authority they work for in order to gain money and celebrity. Steadily, these shows are intoxicating our youth with the thrill of chance, while the more life-fulfilling work of genuine risk awaits.

It reminds me of the Roman Colosseum, where Christians were thrown to lions for sport and gladiators fought to the death to entertain the multitudes, dissipating their thirst for rebellion. Through the use of television and technology, the web of reality shows has inadvertently become our virtual Colosseum, where we are drained of our rightful energy for life and left weary and frustrated, unsure what to do next.

The second fault line around the dissolution of reality involves how acting and pretending have replaced the noble service of actual truth. I remember watching channel five wrestling when I was a kid with my grandfather. He enjoyed it so, though he always knew it was staged. Today, there are many who don't know or care that these versions of life are staged. All this has taken us further into a world that shouts at itself, where we can no longer make the distinction between what is real and what is pretend.

This thinning loss of reality began forty years ago when an actor became president. Then, a wrestler became the governor of Minnesota and a bodybuilder became the governor of California. In 2016, a reality TV host became president. And while Ronald Reagan, Jesse Ventura, and Arnold Schwarzenegger left the world of acting to serve in the actual world of government, Donald Trump brazenly brought the world of pretense like a hammer to the real world, relentlessly inserting and insisting on lies and falsehoods.

From Ronald Reagan, who became president in 1981, to Donald Trump, who finally left office in 2021, the chasm between what is real and what is false has drastically widened. And when all the connections to relationship, nature, history, and tradition are cut, then intensity is mistaken for reality. Without any connection, we suffer groundlessness and reach for the charge of anything in lieu of meaning. Seeking the charge of intensity becomes another form of addiction.

The humanitarian David Addiss confirms that "Both the spiritual traditions and evolutionary biology teach us that turning away from reality leads to suffering and extinction." So, if we are interested in finding each other again and living the one life we are given to the fullest, we need to navigate through this house of mirrors that keeps us from the things that matter. And so, our ability to re-find truth and meaning becomes even more crucial. For once we lose the distinction between what is real and what is false, it is twice as hard to find our way.

## The Loss of a Common Center

Given the loss of relationship embedded in our modern society since the industrial revolution, along with the isolation of technology, and the slow but steady dissolution of reality, the inadvertent effect of social media on our private and public consciousness cannot be overstated. The acceleration of our social crazing and interpersonal collapse has been immensely torqued by the psychological tsunami of social media.

This is made powerfully evident by the bracing and illuminating documentary *The Social Dilemma* (2020, thesocialdilemma.com), directed by Jeff Orlowski and featuring former executives and platform designers from Facebook, Twitter, Google, Instagram, YouTube, and Apple, including Tristan Harris, Jeff Seibert, Bailey Richardson, and thirty others.

The very first social media sites were Six Degrees (1997) and Friendster (2002), followed by Myspace (2003), Facebook (2004), and Twitter (2006). In just twenty years, the relentless narrowing of algorithms has severely isolated the world for individuals, leaving us only with our predilections and fears.

Driven by an extreme sense of greed, these platforms automatically keep refining the content any one individual is exposed to. The unintended impact has been the elimination of any common, agreed-upon foundations. Based on our personal responses, we are clicked into a corner of reality. For instance, if I click on progressive websites,

I am fed only progressive websites and products, including a selective array of news outlets. If I click on conspiracy theories, I am fed only conspiratorial websites, products, and news outlets.

An over-personalized horizon is constructed for everyone. If you were to google "climate change," there would be no common factual definition. If your history of clicks is progressive, you will receive a definition describing climate change as "an existential crisis of our times." But if your history of clicks is conservative, you will receive a definition describing climate change as "an unfounded hoax."

Over time, the effect of over-personalizing our sense of reality is debilitating. The *American Journal of Epidemiology* (2017) reported through a five-thousand-person study that higher social media use correlates with self-reported declines in mental and physical health and life satisfaction. And *The New York Times* (2019) found that the number of countries with political disinformation campaigns on social media has doubled in the past two years. Even Facebook revealed in an internal report (2018) that 64 percent of the people who joined extremist groups on the platform did so because the algorithms steered them there.

Over the years, the drive of social media has created an impenetrable, idiosyncratic bubble for each person. And so, the dissolution of a common agreed-upon reality is now almost complete. Consider how the many facets of a prism are informed by a central light passing through that center into many directions. This represents the health and power of diversity which depends on the kinship of a common center. But removing that common center and only feeding people what they already long for and fear has created a society in which we have become endlessly disconnected facets of a prism with no center. How to break this insidious cycle of separation is becoming the challenge of our age.

## Narcissism versus Inclusion

All of this is made worse by the entrenchment of our self-centeredness as a way of life. One of the hallmarks of Western culture has been its rugged individualism, which at its best has sourced our resilience in the face of adversity. But the aberration of self-reliance has evolved into the modern psychological disease known as narcissism, in which an individual can only perceive and experience life through a relentless self-interest. A narcissist will, in fact, use others like food or fuel, to sustain their own needs at any cost. There is no reciprocity with a narcissist, no relationship at all.

This is yet another way we become rigid and self-contained. For when we only listen to our own thoughts, judgment becomes a toxic way to minimize the truth of others. And the arrogance of certainty only keeps us to ourselves. It muffles the cries of life and dehumanizes others. The inner narrowing of life needed to maintain our self-centeredness matches the outer narrowing of life propagated by the influence of social media. The more self-centered we become, the less tolerant we are. The more desperate the loss of our worth, the more violent our obsession with pushing away and even destroying anything different than us.

Along with the other conditions I've mentioned, the epidemic of narcissism has created an agitated society of lost individuals who behave like cancer cells. In the same way that a diseased cell eats the body that is its host, the narcissistic citizen defies everything and everyone that doesn't validate them while living at the expense of the whole.

Despite all this, it remains true that the antidotes to narcissism are empathy and inclusion. Better, then, to admit that we are lost and hurting. Better to use all the flags and manifestoes as blankets, no matter what is on them. Better to keep each other warm and be humbled by the ways we fall, so we can remember that we are, at heart, the same.

## The Addiction to Violence

The last sixty years have also desensitized us to violence. Brutality has been ingrained in modern life by the proliferation of violence in our movies and video games, as well as the 24/7 news cycle that repeats images of violence ad nauseum. During this period, we have moved from seeing violence as entertainment to experiencing violence as a drug to holding violence, somehow, as a sacred right. From the inception of the National Rifle Association in New York City in 1871, we have steadily moved from holding guns as symbolic of our protection of freedom to holding guns as essential to freedom to equating violence as part of our experience of freedom.

Strangely and tragically, the insurrectionists who violently stormed the US Capitol building on January 6, 2021, seemed both crazed and detached. They were, at once, wildly destructive while merrily documenting their violence on video with cell phones, as if they were watching themselves lose control in a video game.

Our addiction to violence keeps deepening. Twenty years ago, in 2002, the World Health Organization (WHO) issued its first *World Report on Violence and Health.* In the sample year 2000, about 1.6 million people in the world lost their lives to violence. About 320,000 of these deaths were the result of armed conflicts; about 528,000 were from homicides; but almost 800,000 were from suicide. In other words, more than twice as many people worldwide died by their own hand that year than by war.

In 2017, the *Global Burden of Disease* study reported that more than 405,000 people died worldwide from homicide. This was three times the number killed in armed conflict and terrorism combined. And in 2019, the WHO updated their worldwide research, calculating that about 800,000 people still commit suicide annually, which means that a person takes their own life every forty seconds. In other words, the equivalent of half the population of Manhattan is in such pain and so dissatisfied with life that they kill themselves—annually. What does this say about the dislocation, pain, and loneliness of modern life? What deeper remedies does this call forth in us?

While biological inoculation creates antibodies and builds our immunity to disease, individuals and communities are challenged to discover a social inoculation to alienation and violence by inhabiting practices that will keep us awake to the precious unrepeatable quality of life. Such practices from all traditions invigorate our resistance to the isolation and numbness that enable violence. And just as some diseases require booster shots to keep the body immune over time, we must inhabit the deeper practices of being human or else we will fall back into the disconnection that breeds violence.

Charles Dickens began his novel *A Tale of Two Cities* with the sentence, "It was the best of times, it was the worst of times. . . ." Every era, every generation, every day is the best of times and the worst of times. And it is up to us to choose, as those before us, between love and fear.

If we look at humanity as one global body, then, as in every human body, there are healthy cells and toxic cells. Health in the world abounds when there are more healthy individuals than toxic ones. And every time we meet in kindness and truth, we strengthen the immune system of the global body. Since everything is connected, everything matters, and every time you strengthen a heart, you lessen fear and violence somewhere in the world. This, too, is the challenge of our time: to strengthen our hearts and to lessen our fear and violence. We are all in this together, no matter what we believe or where we live.

## The Original Trespass

Underlying all these social fractures is the dark and festering wound in the soul of America that is racism. We have never fully healed the original trespass and brutality of slavery. The first slave ship arrived in the colony of Virginia in 1619. Its name was *White Lion* and it was owned by Robert Rich, Earl of Warwick. And for 403 years, the true reach of freedom has never been completely fulfilled because white America has never relinquished its want to be superior.

The truth is that ever since the founding fathers created a free nation while owning slaves, America has been twisting in a moral tension between bending the world to our will and loving the world. And when we bend the world without loving it, we start to value things over people, and, divorced enough from our true nature, we keep our knee on the neck of others until they can't breathe.

This brings us to the murder of innocent black men and women. In particular, on May 25, 2020, George Floyd, a forty-six-year-old black American man, was killed in Minneapolis, Minnesota, during an arrest for allegedly using a counterfeit bill. Derek Chauvin, a white police officer, knelt on Floyd's neck for nine minutes and twenty-nine seconds while Floyd was handcuffed and lying facedown, begging for his life and repeatedly uttering, "I can't breathe." Officers J. Alexander Kueng and Thomas Lane further restrained Floyd, while officer Tou Thao prevented bystanders from intervening. During the final four minutes, Floyd was unconscious and had no pulse while Chauvin ignored pleas from onlookers to remove his knee, which he wouldn't do until medics told him to.

This travesty reverberated around the world, leading to ongoing protests in more than two hundred cities in the United States and in over sixty countries on nearly every continent. All this during a global pandemic. While we have been forced by the coronavirus to stop our way of life and isolate even further, this groundswell around the world surfaced a felt recognition that we are each other. In spite of the current breakdown in society, our common kinship, in certain ways, is rising through the breaks. It is palpable.

Still, the modern burden of systemic racism is pernicious and undeniable. There is a constant trail of souls of color who are murdered in America by police using excessive force. In 2019, more than $300 million was paid by taxpayers nationwide in financial settlements for police misconduct. Yet only three of ninety-eight officers arrested for fatal on-duty shootings between 2005 and 2018 were convicted of murder.

The wound of racism never seems to heal completely because of our refusal to accept our common kinship at a soul level. Though, it seems we are at another crossroads between love and fear, decency and cruelty, and acceptance and intolerance. Recently, Eddie Glaude, the distinguished professor of African American studies at Princeton, said, "A version of America is dying. We hear its death rattles, loud and violent. But a new America is desperately trying to be born. We are its midwives."

Examples of courage and pain are everywhere. Consider how,

on September 4, 2020, during the tide of worldwide protests against police brutality, Doc Rivers, the then coach of the Los Angeles Clippers, teared up at a news conference and said, "We're the ones getting killed. . . . We're the ones that were denied to live in certain communities. We've been hung. We've been shot. All you do is keep hearing about fear. It's amazing to me why we keep loving this country, and this country does not love us back. It's really so sad."

It is a law of spiritual physics, like gravity, that when we are broken open, we are touched in our core. Then, when we truly feel another's pain, we are experiencing the legacy of all pain. And in receiving the horror of those nine minutes and twenty-nine seconds during which George Floyd was murdered by four police officers, four hundred years of oppression were felt, however briefly, all over the world. I think, in part, because the pandemic has broken humanity open. And despite the social fractures, at least for now, such deep trespass is not just an idea but a felt experience.

The disease and the cure are always close to each other, as night is to day, if we can make it through. As the protests swelled around the world, I was deeply heartened by the courage of our young people. In facing a history of violation, they exemplify who Martin Luther King Jr. imagined when he said, "I believe what the self-centered have torn down, the other-centered will build up."

So much depends on our courage to face the truth and keep loving each other. In the avian world, birds remap their community every day by how they hear each other sing at the first sign of light. And when voices all over the world rise on behalf of each other, we begin to remap society. In the midst of all the chaos and suffering, we can collapse further or we can break the ground of a new age. If we can keep the truth of what we've done to each other in the open, we can begin to rewrite our social contract.

## The Three Questions

We need to break the trance of these social crazings. We need to discover and uncover antidotes to these societal faults: How do we break the isolation of technology and restore our sense of direct relationship? How do we reconnect the fractured parts of our human nature? How do we welcome other views and re-establish a clear and common sense of reality? How do we break our self-centeredness and our addiction to violence? How do we finally heal the wound of racism? And how do we regain our connection to everything larger than us? Whatever conversations and practices can support these social rehabilitations, these are the therapies we need going forward.

So, must we start all over again? Apparently so. It seems each generation takes its turn, trying to churn light from dark and peace from suffering. Until the next kindness is born, remembered, and relied upon. As it is, these social fractures have caused many of us to spin harshly out of control. And the grip of one singular idea, no matter what it is, cannot replace our connection to the web of life. Intensity is not a substitute for kinship. Yet, there is hope. For throughout the human journey, great love and great suffering have always scoured us of our differences and returned us to the common well in which we know what it means to be alive and to live together.

Still, where do we start? It helps to remember that when things break down or don't go as planned, there are always three archetypal questions we are called to ask ourselves: What needs to be repaired? What needs to be reimagined? And what needs to be left dismantled? These questions are always relevant, especially today. For living continually requires repair, and being stopped gives us the chance to reimagine certain things better. And perhaps most crucial is the chance to realize which ways have failed and should never be put back together.

While this tangle of conditions is overwhelming, we are not the first to break apart and come together. The human tribe has been here before, in different iterations. And, as insidious as the recurring devolution has been is as steadfast as the recurring impulse to repair. After the devastation at Hiroshima, those who could walk began to clear the rubble. And when the Nazis fell, sanitation workers in Warsaw led the Jews they had hidden out of the cold, dark sewers. In Rwanda, strangers were appointed to listen to the pain of others.

They sat in the bloodied fields and rocked each other. And four days after the insurrection at the Capitol building in Washington, DC, over two hundred veterans and volunteers spent hours picking up debris and removing hateful stickers left behind by the rioters. And just last week, an elderly woman gave blood because she could. Even toddlers share bits of their egg if they sense another nearby is distressed.

It's been a long road to where we are. Yet, every so often, across the expanses of time, a mountain remakes itself, a forest clears itself, and the ocean reshapes its shore. And once in a generation or two, humanity remakes itself, such as we are right now. And such a remaking is both profound and painful.

But here we are, being asked to put aside our old hypocrisies and all the ways we have pushed each other away. Here we are, being asked to be fierce and tender in our call to love each other until justice and healing are the same thing. Just how do we participate in this remaking of humanity? I think one heart at a time, one truth at a time, one kindness at a time. And we can begin by remaking ourselves.

When the storms have passed, we can begin by discerning what needs to be repaired, what needs to be reimagined, and what needs to stay dismantled. Then, we can start to clear the rubble, to come out of hiding, to listen to the pain of others, to rock each other in the open, and give to those in distress because we can. But the health of generations depends on our efforts and everyday choices—*now*—to accept what we have done and to reclaim the gift of our humanity.

> *Every time we meet in kindness and truth, we*
> *strengthen the immune system of the global body.*

## Questions to Walk With

- Ask yourself in this moment in your life: What needs to be repaired, what needs to be reimagined, and what needs to be left dismantled?

Describe each and what an initial step toward each effort might look like.

- In conversation with a friend or loved one, explore one specific way you can break the isolation of technology and restore your sense of direct relationship, and one specific way you can welcome other views and re-establish a clear and common sense of reality.

# The Nature of Storms

It is only during a storm that a tree knows how strong it is.

—Matshona Dhliwayo

If we are to survive storms, we must understand the nature and life of storms, how they develop, travel, and dissolve, as well as the forms of disturbance they can cause. Looking at the life of actual storms can give us clues to how to meet the many personal, relational, and societal storms we encounter. Often, the storms of life upend us without notice. Yet, like it or not, storms are also agents of transformation.

Though storms can be harsh teachers, they often clear the way, making us drop all that is nonessential. In short, storms make us get real fast. In time, they often show us a way through. In his famous haiku, the seventeenth-century samurai Masahide, who put down his sword to become a poet and study with the master Basho, captured the humbling power of having the way cleared, when he said:

> My barn having burnt
> to the ground, I can see
> the moon more completely.

While there is no bypassing the loss and grief of having lost his barn, the storm and the fire it caused opened Masahide to a vastness he had not yet known. This reveals a paradox we all meet at some point in our journey, which is: we are called to face the loss that being alive initiates, while staying open to whatever we can see more completely once what contains us or preoccupies us has fallen away.

When broken open, we are led to a deeper, more resilient truth, which is: what opens us is never as important as what is opened. What opens us might be unjust or catastrophic. And while the injustice or tragic event might warrant our moral and inner fortitude, the path opened within us and between us is always more important, for it is by following that path that we grow more deeply into our lives.

A poem of mine tries to speak to this:

### Fighting the Instrument

Often the instruments of change
are not kind or just
and the hardest openness
of all might be
to embrace the change
while not wasting your heart
fighting the instrument.

The storm is not as important
as the path it opens.
The mistreatment in one life
never as crucial as the clearing
it makes in your heart.

This is very difficult to accept.
The hammer or cruel one
is always short-lived
compared to the jewel
in the center of the stone.

When mistreated or wronged, we can become distracted by the legitimate quest for validation and justice, which may or may not happen. All the while, the clearing made in our life is waiting for us to enter it. One of the steadfast gifts of friendship is how we can guide each other to that clearing, no matter what may be keeping us away.

Once facing the storm and accepting what it is doing to us, we are often shown a way through. When pained and unsure of the way, I often turn to this anonymous Japanese saying from the fourteenth century:

> All tempest has, like a navel,
> a hole in its middle, through
> which a gull can fly,
> in silence.

More than searching for a map that will lead us to that peaceful center, we are inevitably worn to it, if we can help each other survive the forces that ironically encircle that quiet patch in the center of all storms.

Accepting the greater expanse of life that is waiting beyond whatever is broken, being willing to pursue the cleared way that is opened, and surrendering to the peaceful center we are worn to—these are archetypal passages that souls have always had to climb through in order to survive storms. Exploring these passages and the heartwork necessary to find the strength to meet adversity is what the rest of this book is devoted to.

## How Storms Form

So, let's examine the nature and life of storms for their lessons. First off, a storm is defined as any disturbed state in an environment that disrupts, sometimes fatally, the normal patterns of life in that environment. The word *storm* comes from the German *sturmaz*, meaning "noise, tumult." The word *tumult* refers to "a condition of confusion or disorder." You can readily see that a condition of confusion or disorder can occur within a person as well as between people. That is, storms can appear on all levels—environmental, societal, emotional, mental, and spiritual.

Over the centuries, all the spiritual traditions have developed rituals and practices designed to clear confusion and disorder. Regardless of your upbringing or religious training, I urge you to consider these diverse rituals and practices as tools you can gather to help you both survive and thrive. For, essentially, our individual spiritual practice is comprised of the inner and inter-personal tools we can rely on to clear confusion and disorder. Though, even when we can survive them, storms will come again. For, hard as they can be, they are part of the cycle of nature.

Geological storms require three basic ingredients in order to develop: moisture, unstable air, and lift. The cylinder of a storm is created when a center of low pressure is surrounded by a system of high pressure. These opposing forces create winds and dark, turbulent clouds. The more common types of storms include: hailstorms, ice storms, snowstorms, thunderstorms, windstorms, hurricanes, and tornadoes.

Now, there are storms we encounter and storms we create, such as the turbulence we are now experiencing in our society. Given the storms we encounter, we must learn how to endure their forces, and how to process our grief at what has been lost, while repairing what can be repaired once the storms have gone. But given the storms we create, there is an added responsibility to understand how we became so volatile and destructive, so we can rehabilitate our storm-like tendencies and prevent being so volatile and destructive going forward.

## What Storms Do

There are many forms of storm disturbance. Each affects us differently. With the increase in massive hurricanes, we are very familiar with storm surges, where water levels rise so drastically and powerfully that life as we know it is flooded. In the same way, the overwhelming surge of information and misinformation floods us daily. Unchecked surges of water can lay waste to our homes. Similarly, unchecked surges of media can flood our minds and hearts, causing chaos.

If the water surge is powerful and sustained enough, the coast involved will suffer erosion. Many cities like New Orleans and Charleston are building levees and seawalls to preserve the foundation of their harbors. Likewise, the repetition of strong, untreated storms—such as racism, ethnocentrism, xenophobia, and the generalized fear of others—can erode our foundation. And so, it's imperative to create the social and psychological forms of levees and seawalls that can preserve our communities.

When roads become impassable, we lose our way. And when the surge of confusion and disorder in our lives is relentless, the paths as we know them are no longer accessible. Then, like every generation before us, we have to find a way to work together to repair our impassable roads and to find or create new ones. This is perennial work.

Blizzards and ice storms bring their own travails. The effect of a heavy blizzard is that our vision is impaired and we can't see where we are or where we are going. In whiteouts, there is no depth perception and we lose all context of where we are in relation to others and the environment around us. And in the blizzard or whiteout of one point of view, we lose all depth and context of what is true.

Ice storms are particularly crippling. For the unfettered cold can literally encase us until we suffer a severe form of isolation. Eventually, without any warmth, we begin to go numb until we lose consciousness and drift off. This, too, echoes the cold encasement of technology that, for all its noise, cuts us off from ourselves and others until, before we realize it, we go numb, losing consciousness as we drift off with our cell phones frozen in our grip.

One of the most strident and destructive forms of storm disturbance is cloud-to-ground lightning, which occurs when two charged regions attempt to equalize their energy, causing the release of as much energy as possible. The intensity of the release can be destructive to the regions involved and anything in the path of that release.

As such, lightning can ignite wildfires, just as confused states among people can spark eruptive conflicts that can start fires among us, damaging anything or anyone in their path. During these polarized and strident times, we are experiencing social lightning in which charged regions among us are erupting, causing riots and random acts of violence, including the infamous January sixth insurrection at the United States Capitol and the 693 mass shootings in the United States in 2021.

All this to say that we need the skills and tools, from any source we can find, to shore up our foundation, to repair the paths between us and to find new ones, to outlast the whiteout of any one point of view, and to provide each other enough warmth to thaw the encasement of technology. And most pressing, what are the interpersonal and societal lightning rods that can safely release the intensity of the charged regions of our society?

## How Storms Dissolve

Just how, then, do storms run their course? How do they dissolve and dissipate? Eventually, when the downdrafts in the storm cloud become stronger than the updrafts, the storm starts to weaken. Then, the cloud begins to disappear and the storm dies out with light rain. This points to a timeless law of Spirit, which is: when the forces that ground us are greater than the forces that incite us, the storm, whatever it is, starts to dissipate. Because the storm no longer has a steady supply of unstable air.

In just this way, we quiet storms—personally, relationally, and societally—by reducing the instability in the people and environment around us, by reducing the forces that incite us, and by addressing the concerns at the heart of the storm in an authentic and grounded way. Again, we are not the first to face these challenges, and so, there are countless wisdom sources to help us quiet the situation, ourselves, and each other.

## The Mythology of Storms

Storms exist beyond the Earth, such as solar storms that flare in the sun. The Great Red Spot on Jupiter is an anticyclone that is larger than the Earth. It has been an active storm for at least 356 years, having first been sighted by Galileo. This massive storm is a relentless high-pressure region in the atmosphere of Jupiter. The Great Red Spot is evidence that if the high-pressure that feeds a storm is not addressed and mitigated, it will be impossible for life to exist in that region. We are living in the midst of high-pressure regions in our society, which, if not mitigated, will make it impossible for us to live together here on Earth.

But none of this is new. We have struggled with the power of storms running through our lives since the beginning of time. The bible tells the story of Noah and his charge to build an ark in order to survive the great flood sent by God to eradicate the high-pressure regions of humanity at that time. The *Epic of Gilgamesh,* our oldest narrative, tells a similar story of a flood sent by the gods to force humanity to begin again. When the storms get too big and unwieldy, both within us and between us, we are always asked to begin again.

Every culture has a storm god who is both feared and prayed to. In Greek mythology, Aeolus is the keeper of winds, squalls, and tempests. In Roman lore, it is Jupiter. In Japan, it is Raijin. In China, it is Leigong. In the Celtic way, it is Taranis. In the Yoruba tradition of Africa, it is Oya. And most well-known is the Norse storm god, Thor.

Some cultures have storm gods who are both destructive and beneficial by turns, which affirms that the powerful energy of storms can be channeled toward bringing us together rather than breaking us apart. How can we do this? The rest of this book is exploring how.

In Egyptian mythology, Set is the cataclysmic storm god, while Horus is the gathering storm god. In Hindu mythology, Indra is capable of stirring storms to break the stubbornness of humans, but he is also the god of connections. And we are pointedly challenged today to find a way to gather rather than destroy and to connect rather than be stubborn.

In the ancient Mayan culture of South America, Huracan is the storm god whose name means "one-legged." The modern term *hurricane* might be a cognate of the Mayan name Huracan. But the Mayan storm god is also referred to as U K'ux Kaj, the "Heart of Sky," who is one of the Mayan creators. These Egyptian, Hindu, and Mayan storm gods reveal that the same forces that create life can destroy it, if misused. And each soul on Earth carries the recurring choice between creation and destruction. This, too, is perennial work: to quiet the storms within us and between us, so we can join life rather than separate it.

In medieval Europe, there were traveling magicians known as Tempestarii. Like Native American shamans, they would perform rituals to invoke storms or to chase them away. The hard truth, today, is that we have more than our share of traveling magicians who are stirring storms between us. What we need is to reimagine the ways we can dissipate and ground the storms of our time.

## What Awaits Us

The old question "Is the glass half-full or half-empty?" discerns if we are optimistic or pessimistic at any given time. But the deeper response is that it is always both. And more than our argument between light and dark or miracle and tragedy, we need to face both, embrace both, and accept both—if we are to truly live. For the great challenge of our time is how to let in both the beauty and devastation that meet us every day without wasting our life energy running from one to the other. The real work is in opening our heart wide enough and deep enough to receive both, so we can draw strength from the miracle of life to repair the tragedy of life. This deeper practice is crucial to how we survive storms. How do we dilute the pain of the world in the small cup of peace we brew?

In facing and navigating the storms of human existence, alone and together, we must find and inhabit the resources that will help us:

- learn how to endure the storms we encounter, and how to process our grief at what has been lost to these storms, while repairing what can be repaired once the storms have gone,
- discover and become skilled at rituals and practices designed to clear the confusion and disorder that live within us and around us,

- rehabilitate our own storm-like tendencies to prevent being so volatile and destructive going forward,
- shore up and preserve our foundations from being eroded and washed away,
- work together to repair our impassable roads and to find or create new ones,
- outlast the whiteout of any one point of view so we can retain our depth perception,
- provide each other enough warmth to thaw the encasement of technology,
- create the interpersonal and societal lightning rods that can safely release the intensity of the charged regions of our society,
- inhabit the forces that ground us more than the forces that incite us,
- accept the greater expanse of life that is waiting beyond whatever each storm breaks,
- pursue the cleared way that is opened by each storm,
- and surrender to the peaceful center we are worn to that waits in the center of all storms.

To uncover these resources is the aim of this book. So that we may become the traveling magicians of our day, conjuring ways to dissipate and ground the storms that await us.

*Often, the storms of life upend us*
*without notice. Yet, like it or not, storms are*
*also agents of transformation.*

## Questions to Walk With

- In your journal, describe a time when a storm you encountered cleared an unexpected path for you. Describe the pain in losing what the storm cleared and the new life that the unexpected path led you to. How do you hold both parts of this experience?

- In conversation with a friend or loved one, have each of you describe a storm that you have carried within yourself. What conditions formed it? What path did it take? Was anyone hurt by its disturbance? What did this storm teach you about yourself?

# The Purpose of Goodness

READING NEIL DEGRASSE Tyson, I was stunned to learn by what a thin margin we are here at all. Before the galaxies formed, matter and antimatter ate each other up. And only when a billion-and-one photons outlasted a billion hadrons was the one remaining atomic speck given the chance to seed the living Universe. Had this irrepressible moment swayed the other way, there would have been no galaxies or solar system or planet Earth.

And if the Earth, when forming, had settled any closer to the sun, the oceans would have evaporated. Yet had the Earth settled any farther from the sun, the oceans would have frozen. Too close or too far and there would have been no life on Earth. There would have been no history, no ebb and flow of civilization, nothing to submit to or resist. No chance to be born when we were. No chance to inhabit our individual lives. No chance to meet as we did and fall in love. No chance for me to almost die from cancer. No chance to be worn to a filament of care. None of this has to be as it is. Which is why I wake, every day, compelled, not toward any goal, but to fulfilling this recurring chance to be at all.

This initiation of the Universe has stayed with me: how the immensity of life in the beginning was so dependent on the smallest speck of positive energy. And then, it occurred to me that this is not just a description of the beginning of the Universe, but a description of an *ongoing creation.*

Remarkably, we are here by the one gesture that outweighs all the rest. And this process is never done. That one gesture has to be enlivened and reasserted every day. This is the purpose of goodness: to outweigh all the other possibilities by one gesture of care, so that life will continue. We are challenged to be the one positive ion of energy, the one photon, that ensures that life will have its chance.

This constant unfolding of matter over antimatter is a physical manifestation of the eternal unfolding of love over fear, which can also be understood as the unfolding of interdependence over self-interest. Every day, in every situation, we are called to make the one gesture that will outweigh all the rest. We are called to re-create the Universe by choosing love over fear, by choosing interdependence over self-interest, by choosing care over brutality. And so, ultimately, everything we do matters.

The push and pull between matter and antimatter is endless. A powerful example of this showed itself during Hurricane Irma, which devastated the Caribbean and the southern states of Florida, Georgia, and South Carolina in September 2017.

Within twenty-four hours, we saw both the matter and antimatter of our humanity. As the category-five hurricane whipped its way through the Caribbean, thirty-five residents on the island of St. Thomas were stranded after a ship contracted by Marriott Hotels refused to allow non–hotel guests to board. Although the boat had thirteen hundred open seats, the hotel chain refused to take people who were not Marriott guests. Marriott blamed the St. Thomas Port Authority. But either way, there is your hadron, a coarse example of fear and self-interest spawning brutality.

Cody Howard, one of those left behind, posted on Facebook that

Marriott has just left us on the dock in St. Thomas. They had hundreds of seats still on board but since we didn't have a Marriott reservation, we weren't allowed on the boat. . . . They

called the CEO and he said they didn't want the liability. . . .
Most of these people don't have anywhere to go and now we
are stranded at the Port. . . . They denied humanitarian aid to
women, elderly people, and children.

Shortly after this cruel withholding, an inspiring photon of care
countered the life-draining hadron of self-interest in the form of Delta
flight 431, which was leaving LaGuardia Airport in New York City. Despite the approach of 180-mile-per-hour winds, flight 431 was heading
for San Juan, Puerto Rico, to make one last effort to fly people out.

Once landing, the plane refueled while quickly boarding as many
passengers as possible. It then began taxiing, now as flight 302, waiting to take off from San Juan. By this point, the heft of the storm
and its eye were still to the east of the runway where the Delta flight
would take off. But the hurricane's arm was reaching around to
the west, leaving the plane just a narrow, storm-free window to fly
through before the eye zeroed in on the island.

With stunning resolve, the plane flew through this narrow gap
in the storm, rescuing all they could. Their persistent care was the
one gesture of goodness that outweighed the cruelty of the Marriot
debacle. Flight 302 and the people who flew it and those who helped
it depart and land were, for that day, the one ion of matter that kept
the Universe going.

In truth, we are both: the photon and the hadron, the kindness
that gives and the fear that withholds. It is interesting that *photon*
from the Greek means "light" and *hadron* from the Greek means
"thick, heavy." This affirms the timeless notion, offered in many traditions, that what is life-giving is transparent and luminous and what
is life-draining is opaque and isolating.

Thus, when clear and authentic, when facing what is ours to face,
we are healthy enough and light enough to love the world into to-
morrow. But when knotted and in hiding, when putting other life
down to prop ourselves up, when pushing other life away to run
from what we fear, then we collapse into ourselves and, through our

thickness and heaviness, we engender cruelty. Collapsed into ourselves, we jeopardize life on Earth.

There is one more dangerous position in all of this—the insidious buildup of indifference and neutrality. When we look more closely at the construction of matter, we see that one neutron is necessary in every atom as a stabilizing force between a proton and an electron. However, the stark subatomic reality is that an excess of neutrons destabilizes an atom, basically blowing it apart.

When we translate this to the human journey, it warns us that an excess of neutral or passive souls will create the conditions for a society to become radioactive and toxic.

Martin Niemöller (1892–1984) serves as a powerful example of toxic indifference. A Lutheran pastor born in Germany, Niemöller held anti-Semitic views before World War II, but opposed the Nazification of German churches and for this was imprisoned in several concentration camps until 1945. After being released, he expressed his deep regret for not having done enough to help the victims of the Nazis. He is known for this poem:

> They came first for the Communists,
> and I didn't speak up because I wasn't a Communist.
> Then they came for the Jews,
> and I didn't speak up because I wasn't a Jew.
> Then they came for the trade unionists,
> and I didn't speak up because I wasn't a trade unionist.
> Then they came for the Catholics,
> and I didn't speak up because I was a Protestant.
> Then they came for me,
> and by that time no one was left to speak up.

Niemöller can be seen as a passive neutron who, along with so many indifferent Germans, enabled the release of unprecedented violence throughout Nazi Germany and then the world.

Ultimately, we are not masters of life, but servants brought alive by our service. And whether we manipulate or serve makes all the difference. And so, the very health of our humanity depends on the authenticity and care of its souls.

That so much depends on so little is the cornerstone of faith, not faith in an idea or a doctrine, but deep-seeded functional faith, which calls on us to believe in the one gesture we can offer—every day—never knowing if that particular kindness is the one that will keep life going. It may be our impulse to help an old woman pick up her groceries in the parking lot, or sitting for a minute with someone who is beside themselves, or stopping to move a stray dog out of the road.

Every day, there are countless gestures that keep the world going, which are anonymous but deeply essential. So, the next time you witness indifference, selfishness, or cruelty, counter it with a gesture of kindness and care. Be the anonymous photon, the one ion of care that makes life possible, that keeps this mysterious journey alive. Outweigh the dark choices—one more time. Can there be anything more noble and relevant than to dare to be relentlessly kind in an effort to keep life going?

*This is the purpose of goodness: to outweigh all the other possibilities by one gesture of care, so that life will continue.*

## Questions to Walk With

- In your journal, describe a moment of goodness and a moment of withholding that you witnessed during your week. How did each gesture affect the life around you?
- In conversation with a friend or loved one, tell the history of a recent moment of withholding on your part and what made you retreat from life. Then, tell the story of a recent moment of care that you extended and what made you lean so fully into life. What happens to you when you withhold and what happens to you when you care?

Delta Flight 302 flying through Hurricane Irma, Sept. 6, 2017

part 2

# Finding the Strength

❦

We gauge culture by the extent to which a
whole people, not only individuals . . . strive
for spiritual integrity; the extent to which
inwardness, compassion, justice, and holiness are
to be found in the daily life of the masses.

*—Abraham Heschel*

You cannot hope to build a better world
without improving the individuals. To that end,
each of us must work for his [or her]
own improvement, and at the same time share
a general responsibility for all humanity.

*—Marie Curie*

# *Every Path Holds a Question*

———

The sacred is a larger, wilder hill
whose path is often hidden
by all that has grown over it.

—MN

THIS SECTION EXPLORES the resources that will help us:

- accept the greater expanse of life that is waiting beyond whatever each storm breaks,
- pursue the cleared way that is opened by each storm,
- and outlast the whiteout of any one point of view so we can retain our depth perception.

Today, as in other times, there is a baseless controversy about immigration, about who belongs and who doesn't. But everyone on Earth is an immigrant. Each of us, an immigrant from the world of Spirit into bodily form. Each of us, an immigrant from birth to death. And it is belonging itself that is our home, no matter where we are from. It is the acceptance of the journey and the love of those on the journey that shapes us all. It is what we find underneath what is taken that makes us enduring and kind. I was moved to learn that there is a Sufi practice known as *sohbet,* which honors the spiritual talk between friends. This is not just reserved for human friendships, but our friendships with trees, birds, the depths of the ocean; our friendships with the grassy fields of truth and the constant winds of love. Each friendship is a path of immigration into life, if we can meet the unknown as a teacher and not as a catastrophe. And every path holds a question that, if entered, will help reanimate our sense of birth, no matter our wounds. Experience teaches us that the worth of any story is in how it reveals aliveness and relationship. For each person's life is a myth whose wisdom waits for us to unearth the truth our experience carries. The chapters in this section invite you to honor your life as a mystery that deserves all your attention.

# One Candle Lighting Many

A REVEALING QUOTE attributed to Buddha reads, "Thousands of candles can be lighted from a single candle, and the life of the candle will not be shortened." This image affirms that when we give from our center, our ability to give is endless. And so, the mystery of true kindness is that when we give from the depth of our care, we are not diminished but enlivened.

There have been many times in my life when I felt like I had nothing left to give. And just then, though I was exhausted and depleted, I found myself moved to try to give anyway. To my surprise, there has always been something else there. What comes up and through in those moments always seems to be full of life-force. In those brief and intense moments of holding nothing back, I become the one candle lighting many.

So, these questions unfold: How do we keep the singular light within us lit? How do we tend to our locus of care? How do we keep the passageway between us and life open, so our care can enter the world? How do we let that singular, enduring light be our teacher? How do we devote ourselves to the practice of accessing that light and to passing it on to the souls we meet along the way?

I am continually in awe that when we have the courage to face what is before us—in truth with love—what is dark starts to lighten. Part of the human journey is how we are always using our gifts to put things back together. This call is expressed in all cultures. For instance, the Arabic word *we'aam* means "putting back together that which has been broken." And the Hebrew phrase *Tikkun Olam* means "you are here to repair the world."

Here is a compelling example. Born in Poland, Marie Curie (1867–1934) was a brilliant scientist who was the first woman to win a Nobel Prize. In fact, she won two, in 1903 for physics and in 1911 for chemistry. In partnership with her husband, Pierre Curie, their discoveries opened the way to use radiation as a means of medical imaging and as an eventual therapy for cancer.

Once she saw the inherent value in something, she was relentless in making good use of it. Her tireless effort to help the wounded on the front lines of World War I is a stirring case in point. First, she tried to donate her gold Nobel Prize medallions to the war effort, saying, "I am going to give up the little gold I possess. I shall add to this the scientific medals, which are quite useless to me."

But the French National Bank refused them. She pressed on and developed mobile radiography units and ventured with her seventeen-year-old daughter, Irene, to the front lines to x-ray wounded soldiers. She went on to train aides to operate more than twenty mobile units, which saved over a million lives by the end of the war.

However, like Alfred Nobel's discovery of dynamite, Marie Curie's discovery of radium and the effects of radiation led to both beneficial breakthroughs and devastating misuses. Beyond Curie's lifetime, the splitting of the atom led to the creation of nuclear bombs and the careless use of nuclear reactors. We can only imagine her reaction, if she were alive, to the devastation at Hiroshima and Nagasaki in 1945, as well as to the nuclear accident at Chernobyl in 1986. But offsetting the destruction, countless lives have been healed and saved by medical imaging throughout the years and through the pinpoint use of radiation to reduce tumors.

Yet for all her brilliance and accomplishments, I admire her quiet courage to x-ray soldiers in mud-ruined battlefields to prevent needless amputations. Marie Curie was one candle lighting many.

Sadly though—like Icarus, whose wings of wax melted for flying too close to the sun—both Pierre and Marie Curie suffered under-lying illnesses from decades of exposure to radiation, which nei-ther was aware of. Perhaps, this was the cost exacted by the gods for touching life itself at such an elemental level. Like Prometheus, they may have been fated to live with constant pain for giving another form of fire to the rest of us.

In life's journey, we all struggle with versions of withholding that undercut our goodness. And so, another question arises: What makes us give at times and hoard at other times? Consider those giants of opera Giuseppe Verdi (1813–1901) and Richard Wagner (1813–1883), who were born the same year. While Verdi was a good man with an immense heart, Wagner was self-centered and driven by an insatia-ble ego. At the peak of their careers, Verdi funded and built an old-age home for all those who had worked to bring his operas to life, while Wagner built an ornate theater as an edifice to himself.

It seems an irrefutable law of Spirit that just as dark can muffle light, a hardness of heart can muffle kindness. And just as light can enter dark and, from inside it, allow the darkness to dissipate, kind-ness can allow a hardness of heart to soften back into love. Every day, light and dark meet head on to remind us of this. Not once, but twice—at sunrise and sunset. This daily opening and closing of the Universe reminds us that each day we have this choice. Every time a hardness meets a kindness, it can be a dawn or a dusk. Every day, there are these choices: to open or close, to soften or harden, to give or hoard.

We all take turns being hard and giving. And knowing that our gifts are lent to us can change everything. For being a carrier of light can be enlivening, while seeing ourselves as a source of light can be exhausting. As for me, I still believe that the human flower breaks ground regardless of the storm because we are meant to give one more time than take. I have found through the years that the joy is in the work, in the process, in the expression of our care. And we can't pretend, regardless of our cynicism or hope, that we know the outcome. For the process is our teacher.

We have only to look to nature for our model. For as spring

happens every year because of the miracle of pollination, kindness pollinates humanity. And each gesture entered with the full presence of an open heart stitches another rip in the Living Universe. Wisdom is woven from our shared humanity, one giving thread at a time.

*We are always using our gifts to*
*put things back together.*

## Questions to Walk With

- In your journal, describe a time when your heart hardened and, then, a time when your heart softened. What led to each of these instances and what does this tell you about your own rhythms of giving and withholding?
- In conversation with a friend or loved one, tell the story of someone you admire who has been one candle lighting many. What strengths and gifts enabled them to be so giving?

# To Grow What We Know

Education must . . . be not only a transmission of culture but also a provider of alternative views of the world and a strengthener of the will to explore them.

—Jerome Bruner

There have always been two major schools of thought regarding education throughout human history: the effort to confirm and preserve what we already know, and the effort to grow what we know. We move from confirming what we already know to growing what we know by following the spark of truth that waits in our heart. So, a central question to ask repeatedly is: Am I seeking—that is, seeing, listening, writing, painting, thinking, feeling, loving, being, doing—to confirm what I already know or to grow?

Ultimately, knowledge is like fire. It can be an enduring element that lights and warms us as it parts the dark. Or it can destroy everything it touches if spread without care. The difference often resides in whether we handle knowledge with reverence.

The more insecure or off-center we are, the more we labor outwardly to have everything and everyone mirror us. When, often, that insecurity is an indication that we need to go deeper into the ground of our experience in order to renew our direct connection with life. Our inner stability, or lack of it, triggers a psycho-spiritual form of cause and effect. The more insecure we are, the more we need to impose our views on everything and everyone. The more secure we are, the more room we make for other views of life.

So, how do we prepare ourselves to fully experience the web of life? This evokes the practice of being human, which is not telling people how to be in the world, but encouraging individuals to devote themselves to discerning and inhabiting their own journey in getting up when falling down, in lifting themselves out of despair, in returning to a sense of safety when feeling afraid, and in opening up after pain or trauma has closed them down.

In her wise and fiercely loving book *See No Stranger*, the American-born Sikh Valarie Kaur shares how her grandfather, Papa Ji, was constantly cultivating her orientation to wonder. This ancient and timeless openness to life is at the heart of all resilience and needs to be restored as a cornerstone of enduring education. By remaining wholehearted, we stay close to wonder, which helps us endure the trespasses of the modern world, which have their own tangled lineage of fear and withholding. I firmly believe that the functional aim of all education has always been to give one more time than others take, to get up one more time than we fall down, and to open our hearts one more time than the storms of life close them.

For all our effort and willfulness, we are eroded by experience to a common, basic yearning below all our wants and ambitions. And that basic yearning is to simply be here, as fully alive as possible, with no dream other than to breathe and sing. Even when going through difficult, challenging times, even when hurt and confused, we are left with the simple and profound effort to cry out our human names for what is unnamable—the very Source of life, whether you call that God or Life-Force or the Mysterious Power of Nature or any of the thousand names we offer for what gives us life. We are humbly left to breathe and sing as gentle animals, just thankful to be here and to be alive in kinship with each other.

Repeatedly, love and suffering break the trance of single-point thinking. Then, we realize, as Einstein affirmed, that there are many centers and that the web of their connection reveals a Oneness that sustains all life. We participate in this Oneness by being thoroughly ourselves, which leads us to life-changing moments in which we are one with each other and all of existence. Being ourselves until we are one is the relational paradox that is the heartbeat of the Universe. Moments such as when my father, who could no longer speak, stared into Eternity from his hospital bed and I took his hand. Or when my wife, Susan, and I first fell into each other's eyes over twenty-five years ago. Or when I woke from surgery stripped of all pretense. Or when George and I stood on a cliff along the Pacific, the ancient wind making human flags of us.

In truth, the heartwork we each do matters more than ever. For with each act of presence and authenticity, we are keeping the literacy of the heart alive. And every time we listen and care for others, we are re-stitching the fabric of humanity. For holding, listening, the life of questions, and story are the barely seeable threads that keep the world together. Every time you hold or are held, every time you ask a question or tell a story, every time you truly listen to a question or a story, you are weaving or repairing the threads that keep the world together.

And so, if I am loyal, it is to this: to meet everything with care. I try to hold nothing back or in. Like an iris shaking off its dirt to meet the world, I grow by living inside out, nectar first. For living inside out is how the heart educates us until we come alive and are fully here. Time and again, experience confirms that the heart is the central instrument that navigates us through the many currents of being alive.

Repeatedly, we are called to open our heart, no matter what is in the way, so that the deeper unassailable current of life can cleanse us of all sediment until our love of all things returns. We must do this every day. For it is through the continual opening of the heart that life can find itself and renew itself through you and me and all the elements and fragments of the world.

After all this way, I can only say that I am of the lineage that believes that everything in life is connected. How do I know this? I can't really say. I just know that through the thoroughness of my heart, I continue to experience the Oneness of Things, which enlivens and strengthens me. The question is: How can we participate in the

Oneness of Things? For me, it always starts with being real, authentic, and honest, which opens my heart. And with an open heart, I have access, however briefly, to the resources of the Universe. With my mind, I can grasp Oneness, but through my heart, I can inhabit Oneness.

*Living inside out is how the heart educates*
*us until we come alive and are fully here.*

## Questions to Walk With

- In your journal, describe a time when you put effort into confirming what you already know and what led you to do this. And describe a time when you put effort into growing what you know and what led you to do this.
- In conversation with a friend or loved one, discuss your experience of wonder. Describe when you first encountered wonder and what keeps you from it from time to time.

# You Can't Fly with One Wing

Down in their hearts, [the wise] know this truth: the only way to help yourself is to help others.

—Elbert Hubbard

AFTER THE FIRST half of her life was spent in a convent, Catherine of Siena (1347–1380) was called by God to enter the world. She questioned, why? Jesus came to her in a vision and said, "There are two commandments. Love God, and love your neighbor as yourself. You have only done the first. You can't walk with one foot. You can't fly with one wing." And so, she entered the world, aspiring to be an integrated contemplative, loving the God in others and the God in herself until the commandments became interchangeable, until loving others was loving self was loving God, in a series of embodied moments that erased all boundaries.

By knowing herself and loving the world, Catherine aspired to experience an indivisible Oneness of Heart. Hindu sages refer to this Oneness of Heart when they offer the greeting *namaste*. As Ram Dass explains:

In India when we meet and part we often say Namaste, which means: I honor the place in you where the entire Universe resides; I honor the place in you of love, of light, of truth, of peace. I honor the place within you where if you are in that place in you and I am in that place in me, there is only one of us. . . . Namaste.

The promise of the inner world is that the flow of Spirit between the living joins us without restraint and without preference. One way to characterize this is as *generosity* which comes from the Greek *plerosis,* meaning "a fullness that moves in all directions." When we love the very heart of each other, we drink from the fullness that moves in all directions.

Of course, being human and living on Earth, we fall prey to many distractions and disruptions. And so, we must remain committed to finding and drinking from that fullness that moves in all directions, again and again.

The original meaning of the word *repeat,* from the late Middle English, means "to seek again." This is our lifelong practice: to seek the Spirit that flows between us, again and again.

If the soul is a window, how do we keep the window clean? How do we keep the window of the soul open? How do we go outside and still remain inside at the same time? How do we inhabit life fully?

Another way to understand this lifelong quest is not to concentrate on seeking things but to seek how to bring our soul to the soul of others by being who we are everywhere. In essence, we learn to open our eyes in order to see. And we learn to open our heart in order to love. The vow of inner work is to open our eyes and open our heart. The vow of service is to see and love. What good is opening our eyes, if we never see? And what good is opening our heart, if we never love?

## Three Voices

I'd like to explore three voices that speak to how we might live into the Oneness of Heart that Catherine of Siena was called to.

The first voice is William Stafford, the legendary poet of the Northwest, mentor to the great contemporary poet Naomi Shihab Nye.

Stafford said:

> If you don't know the kind of person I am
> and I don't know the kind of person you are
> a pattern that others made may prevail in the world
> and following the wrong god home we may miss our star.

The poet is referring to how we tune to each other by being authentic. If I don't take the time to move toward what is precious in you, and you toward me, then we have no chance of finding the fullness that moves in all directions. We will miss our star, because when we don't lean in to what is authentic and precious, we close our hearts to each other and to the life before us. Then, like water filling a hole, other things will fill us. "A pattern that others made may prevail in the world" and we'll be induced to follow the wrong god home.

The second voice speaks to how we can be awakened in a moment of unravel when, in losing our way, we remember how rare a journey this life is. Before this transformative moment was called a midlife crisis, Dante wrote about it deeply. He opens *The Divine Comedy* with this moment:

> Midway this way of life we're bound upon,
> I woke to find myself in a dark wood,
> where the right road was wholly lost and gone.

The entire *Divine Comedy* begins in this dark confusion. In talking about this archetypal passage, Joseph Campbell says:

What happens to a lot of people is we work very hard and we build a ladder. Then we place the ladder against a wall. Then we start climbing. Somewhere halfway in life, roughly, we realize that it's the wrong wall and that, in fact, maybe we don't even need to be climbing a ladder. Maybe we need to be getting in a boat and paddling out to sea. Or maybe we need to just climb down.

The state of being wholly alive, below the prevailing patterns of the world, is not a state of excellence but a state of connectedness. It's more important to be thorough than perfect. Yes, I want things to be clear when I write or speak. I work on what comes through me that it might ring true. But it's more important to speak the truth roughly than not at all.

Why, then, do we so easily turn away from our star to follow a wrong god home? I think because when the way gets difficult, we misunderstand the human journey. I think we get caught up very easily in thinking that we know what we want and what we need. But when experience stops us and rearranges us, what we want and need and where we're going are not so clear. Despite all our dreams and schemes, we encounter life and, though we want so much, we reach and miss and fall off, only to discover how rare it is to be a Spirit on Earth.

Under all our designs, we're asked to make countless decisions about what it means to be here and how to be fully alive. Along the way, we are constantly distracted by all the goals we reach for, all the patterns that prevail in the world, and all the gods we lean on. In truth, our dreams and strategies give us the illusion that we are entitled to have things go as planned. But predestation is not guaranteed in the human journey.

It was the great Hindu sage Ramana Maharshi who said, "One of the great paradoxes of life is that we keep seeking reality when we, in fact, are reality." This doesn't mean we should not become or reach. Paradoxically, reaching is a means toward a deeper form of being, precisely because, in time, we're broken of what we reach for. This is an important part of the journey. Yet, we are so focused on what we're reaching for that we often miss the lessons along the way, perceiving each failed reach as an inadequacy.

The third voice is Basho, the great Japanese poet of the 1600s who made haiku the meaningful form it is. In one of his emanating haikus, Basho says:

> The temple bell stops,
> but the sound keeps coming
> out of the flowers.

Basho affirms for us that if we keep moving toward what is precious, we will touch into the Oneness of Heart that exists beyond what is initially heard. When the bell is rung and the sound keeps vibrating under the covering of silence, it doesn't mean it's gone. It means our ability to hear it has ceased. Yet, when we can lean toward what is precious with an open heart, we can sense the invisible tones that hold life and us together.

For example, you could say the bell of my father's life has stopped now that he is gone. Yet what I'm starting to feel is the sound of his life coming out of the flowers, moving into a deeper presence that I'm asked to somehow stay open to. Because I still love him, I'm beginning to hear him in the tones that hold everything together.

We are always led beyond our conscious knowing by the many clues the heart will pick up on, if we are open enough to lean in and move toward them. We always have a teacher just around the corner that is asking us to lean a little further into our not-knowing.

## Leaning In

We are left with the never-ending call to know ourselves and love the world, in an effort to experience an indivisible Oneness of Heart as we move through the fullness that moves in all directions. This is what it means to be awake and thorough of heart.

The courage, then, is to keep leaning into life. For the storms of circumstance will toss us far from what is precious. By their very nature, events will bump us along and bruise us. Not because life is evil, but because, like swells in the ocean, the currents will push us to and fro. But we're stronger and more resilient than almost any hurt that can come our way, if we keep moving toward what is precious with a commitment to be caring and real.

*The heartening way* is that when the heart closes, we must vow to open it. When stalled and broken, we must help each other lean into life again and take the risk to say yes. How, then, do we gather strength from how this works, knowing that the next day, more obstacles and storms will stop us and lift us?

When I feel small, I have to enlarge. When I feel distrustful, I have to take the risk to trust again. When I don't know how, I have to ask for help. This is the long road to inner freedom that opens each of us when we can keep saying yes to life, even when we are bruised and fearful.

*When we love the very heart of each other, we drink from the fullness that moves in all directions.*

## Questions to Walk With

- In your journal, describe a time when loving and caring for another enabled you to become more intimate with a part of your own nature.
- In conversation with a friend or loved one, describe the ways you lean into life. What draws your spirit forward into the world?

# Notes on the True Self

WHEN YOUNG, EXPERIENCING the True Self was a measure of how authentic and integral I was. Did I live up to my values? Was I able to consistently return to what matters after falling down? This remains a helpful, unending practice. But over time, I began to learn more about the nature of the True Self and its relationship to the larger, living Universe.

For measuring daily integrity, while essential, is like checking the thermometer every day to know the temperature. It has little to do with our deeper knowledge of the weather and its patterns. After enough experience, I began to wonder about the larger context of life's currents, out of which the True Self emanates.

To explore this, we must begin by asking: What does the True Self refer to? What does it mean? Is there a common sense of self and truth that is useful in our day-to-day quest for congruence and authenticity?

There is a central paradox in having a self that carries some form of Spirit within it. For as human beings, our being is infinite and un-limited, but our humanness is very finite and limited. And so, there is a common, inner tension, as we soar and plod at the same time. The being in us flies like a hawk. It knows nothing of the ground. It sees the terrain but glides above all its obstacles. But the human in us walks like a horse and must climb over everything. It plods along, a step at a time, and must traverse everything in its way.

So, the hawklike Spirit is instantaneous in seeing where we need to go and can fly there directly, while the horselike human in us must walk around the fallen tree and rebuild the bridge in order to cross the river. We suffer this tension between our human and our being constantly. The work of a True Self is to keep our human and our being kindly tethered, so they can work together.

We all experience this mysterious process of being a spirit in a body in time on Earth, which all the traditions try to name, the way pilgrims on different shores offer different names for the same constellation they see at night. But the mysterious process of life remains as unnamable as it is steadfast.

Of the many names and frames the various traditions offer, it helps to begin with how the Hindu worldview describes our long walk through time. There is an ancient trinity of eternal forces known as Brahma, Vishnu, and Shiva. Brahma is the irrepressible, continuous life-force that informs everything. Vishnu represents the life of forms which carries this life-force in infinite variety. And since the life-force lives forever while the forms eventually die, Shiva is the transforming agent by which the forms dissolve so that the eternal life-force can return to the formless realm of Brahma, where the process begins again.

No one can escape the spiritual fact that every form of life on Earth comes into being and, in time, will dissolve. And so, we are each a container, holding the portion of Universal Spirit we are born to carry while we are here. Again, the Hindu term *namaste* means "I bow to the portion of Universal Spirit that resides in you." In the West, we call that portion of Universal Spirit that resides in us our soul.

The central questions, then, are: Will you be a good steward of the portion of Universal Spirit you are blessed to carry in the container that is your life—as well as you can, for as long as you can? And what does being a good steward of your soul mean? What does being a good steward of the light you carry look like for you personally?

So, if the Self is a container to carry our portion of Universal Spirit through Time, then the True Self is a sturdy vessel or boat that can be relied on to help us cross the sea of life. And the ego, if properly used, is a steering device—a rudder or steering wheel. Problems arise when we ask the ego to function beyond its natural role. You don't ask a steering wheel where to go, you direct it. Likewise, you don't ask your ego where to go, but consult your heart and Spirit where to go. Then, you can enlist your ego to properly follow your call rather than to lead it.

Guides who have been helpful over the years regarding the nature of the True Self include the Sufi poets Rumi, Kabir, and Hafiz, as well as the psychological giants Carl Jung and Carl Rogers. I have also found great, foundational strength in Walt Whitman's mammoth poem "Song of Myself." In his epic conversation with the Universe, Whitman evolves his own notion of a True Self by constantly calibrating his working relationship with everything living. A great exercise of self-inquiry is to journal your way through "Song of Myself," responding to each of its fifty-seven chapters, as if you are in a long conversation with Whitman himself.

While taking inventory of our character is a good way to measure our daily integrity, the deeper, more lasting practice of the True Self is to discern and sustain our authentic relationships with everyone and everything around us. At this point, it helps to redefine true and false here as whole and partial. When in integrity with our True Self—when in accord with the portion of Universal Spirit we are blessed to carry within us while here—we are whole and enlivened. When not in accord with the life around us, we become limited and partial and suffer being fragmented. Returning to our True Self requires the ability to recognize our patterns of being limited and partial, so we can do what is necessary to restore our aliveness and authenticity.

There are three irrefutable qualities of Spirit—equivalent to the elements of fire, water, and air—that are always available to us. Immersing ourselves in these qualities will help restore us to our True Self. These spiritual qualities are presence, meaning, and relationship, and it helps to develop a personal practice around each.

Presence enables us to restore our direct experience of life. It helps us to re-feel how rare it is to be here at all. From that inhabited sense, we see differently, hear differently, and speak differently. Once re-membering how rare it is to be alive, we make different decisions. All the traditions have practices that invoke presence and, thereby, offer us tools by which to restore our direct experience of life. Being human, we will fall down and forget. We will drop our clarity like a plate in the kitchen and not know how to put it back together. This is the work of presence, to put our True Self back together when expe-rience cracks or breaks our sense of it.

Yet while there can be no sense of authenticity without direct ex-perience, if I am only left with my experience, I will become insular and myopic. For life is so much more than my experience alone. This brings us to the spiritual quality of meaning, whereby we can feel and receive the direct experience and presence of others. While the modern world would have you believe that understanding through the intellect is the only way to grasp meaning, the more deeply felt practices of holding and listening are the more lasting conduits of meaning. And so, the work of meaning is to ensure that our True Self maintains a breathing openness to life outside ourself.

Lastly, there is the spiritual quality of relationship, which weaves the threads that connect everything in the living Universe. Every-thing is in relationship. Nothing is completely isolated. If presence and meaning are the electricity, then relationships are the wires that carry these life-forces.

Each of us is challenged to personalize our connection to the qualities of presence, meaning, and relationship, though no one can tell you how. One way that I try is to maintain three simple vows by which I start each day: I let in light by opening the blinds, I tend to something living by feeding our dog, and I do something for some-one I love by making coffee for my wife, Susan, before she gets up.

When I am present to these small tasks, they let me enter the day with a connection to my True Self, and this changes every-thing. If I rush through these efforts or I'm preoccupied, these ritu-als slip into habits and become meaningless. But this is the work of self-awareness. For when I realize I have rushed through them, I can return and enter them again, more wholeheartedly.

It's instructive to learn that the word *ritual* goes back to the Sanskrit *rta*, which means "visible order." So, in deep and profound ways, ritual makes the order of the Universe visible.

Though the practice and ritual of maintaining a True Self is akin to keeping a tool or instrument clean and sharp, the tool or instrument hasn't fulfilled its purpose until it is used to build or repair something. Similarly, maintaining our integrity and living up to our values keeps the tool of a True Self clean and sharp. But the True Self hasn't fulfilled its purpose until it is put to good use in building or repairing the connections that keep the living Universe together.

Our attempts at love call for us to both care for the self and love others. For, in loving others, we are challenged to stay who we are without walling off others or without drowning in their pain. This is the learning ground of the True Self. For often, when sensitive and caring, we lose who we are and become the suffering of the loved one. Or, overwhelmed, we remove ourselves, putting up a wall in order to maintain who we are. Then, we try to love from a distance. In many ways, the True Self, if honored, is the gateway to compassion.

The learning ground of intimacy is what sharpens the tool that is the True Self. In the Buddhist tradition, this work is embodied in the journey of the Bodhisattva, one who, in experiencing acceptance and equanimity, stays on the journey with those who are suffering and troubled, one who accepts life here on Earth, flawed as it is, in order to work and live with others.

In looking back at the evolution of my own True Self, I was recently drawn to write this poem:

### Praying I Will Find

I used to have so many plans, good plans,
grand plans. In the beginning, I would be
annoyed by the calamities I'd meet along
the way that would keep me from my plans.

I used to pride myself on how I could get
back on track so quickly. But the more I
loved and the more I suffered, the more
my plans were interrupted by those in
need.

Eventually, the call of life, unexpected
and unrehearsed, made swiss cheese of
my plans.

Now, like an emperor undressed by time,
I wander the days naked of plans, praying
that I will find love to give and suffering
to heal before the sun goes down.

Staying true and connected is a humbling journey. And my invitation to those on the way is to follow your heart, which will lead you down unexpected paths, ever closer to the sweet ache of being alive. When I was young, I mistook the sweet ache of being alive for sadness and was miseducated to try to get rid of it, which I couldn't. Then, I tried to quiet it and, failing, I tried to drown it out. It was after almost dying from cancer in my thirties that I realized that the sweet ache of being alive is my oldest friend. It is how I know I am here.

The sweet ache is the tug of the strings that connect everything in the Universe, one of which goes right through our heart. When I am open-hearted and fully present, I feel the tug of the Universe and then I remember how rare it is to be here at all. The sweet ache always returns me to my True Self, which in turn, returns me to my place in the web of all living things.

In reflecting on the notion of a True Self, I leave you with another poem of mine, by which I know I'm on the path:

### The Moment of Poetry

When the sweet ache of being alive,
lodged between who you are

and who you will be,
is awakened,
befriend this moment.
It will guide you.
Its sweetness is what holds you.
Its ache is what moves you on.


*The work of a True Self is to keep our human and*
*our being kindly tethered, so they can work together.*


## Questions to Walk With

- In your journal, describe your sense of your True Self and your history of being in and out of clear contact with it.
- In conversation with a friend or loved one, describe the first time you realized that you had a True Self and how it became known to you.

# The Daily Work of Awareness

WE SPEND SO much time anticipating what will happen next that we often miss the whisper of Heaven that unfolds wherever we are. And though I have known and survived many forms of Heaven and pain, fear is the troll in my mind that anticipates more pain. Just as a loud noise prevents us from finding peace in the center of silence, fear prevents us from finding the inch of Heaven in the center of whatever moment we are in. Yet, no matter how much I've been through and how much I've learned, I can't stop the fearful wave of anticipation. No one can. It is part of being human.

But I can right-size it from time to time. When fully engaged in learning, or caring for another, or in a moment of devotion to all that I believe about the Mystery of Life—in these openings, the fearful anticipation loosens and I am completely present, at least for a while. The practice of authenticity is building on these moments until they open up our days.

I remember during my cancer journey, when my veins had gone brittle from too many needles. The nurse was having trouble inserting an IV for my chemo. She had tried five times and no go. I was sweating in fear of the next try. Each one burned. Then, my dear friend Robert put his hand on my forearm, rubbing the mess of pinpricks. His touch broke my anticipation. I began to cry. And while he rubbed my arm, the nurse tried again.

Ever since, I have used touch and care to interrupt fear. Touch works better than talk to deliver us into the peace that waits in the center of every moment. There, in the well of all time that cradles every struggle, we are carried, the way a broken raft is carried on the surface of the roughest sea.

I know, all these years later, that when afraid of dying, we pour our fear into the nearest happening—a trip to the dentist or a sudden bang in the night. And afraid of living, we hesitate as if the next moment is a ledge we will fall off. But when winded of my cautions, I am blissfully alive wherever I am. Then, the nearest shimmer of life—a bluebird building its nest or a child next door learning how to walk—parts the noise that always covers the fact that this moment is yet to happen. I close my eyes when afraid and open them to remember that life is real. Surmounting the pain of closing and inhabiting the struggle to open is the daily work of awareness, from which no one is exempt.

Here is such a moment. It was during the first year of the pandemic. It was early May. The apple blossoms behind Susan's studio were opening and the weeping cherry was turning pink. We were having coffee on the deck, our faces in the sun. Everything was so peaceful and full of quiet that we could, for the moment, forget that the Earth was being riddled with disease. Still, all things are true and all things are happening at once. As I inhaled the early light, someone was taking their last breath. As I wrestled with a jolt of fear, a couple was making love for the first time. As a thousand things were falling apart, another thousand were coming together. This ebb and flow on a cosmic scale is what keeps the Universe going.

It felt inevitable that the more I couldn't go anywhere, the more my heart began to travel everywhere—across the globe, then back and forth through history. With my face in the sun, I began to think of a daughter holding her father on a cobbled street in London as he was dying from the Black Plague that was brought to Europe by a rodent on a cart along the silk road in China. It crept onto a ship that chopped through the sea to England. Though Philip VI of France swore it was the conjunction of three planets in 1345 that unleashed the pestilence.

So quickly to the Middle Ages and back, as my dog dropped a ball in front of me. The light on the fence was golden and I pondered how gold is melted in fire till it is supple enough to bend and mold. Likewise, it seems so much suffering is needed over a lifetime to make us soft enough to let all of life through. I wish it were different. And certainly, beauty and wonder and love can open us as well. My dog came back for another throw. I wanted to lose myself in this drop of spring before the rest of life could catch up.

Ultimately, our job while here is threefold. First, like a mountain that is steadfast in meeting the elements, we are called to face the wear of time, so we can reflect and endure the truth revealed. Some say this is doing nothing. If so, it is a noble nothing that in time reveals everything.

Second, like a river that is relentless in how it carves its path to the sea, we are called to bring what is true into the world. Some say this is our vigilance for justice. If so, this is a noble doing that in time honors everything.

And third, like a tireless seeker who finds God in the smallest pebble, we are called to care for everything in our way. Some say this is impossible. If so, this is the noblest errand of all—to go nowhere like a mountain and everywhere like a river until we turn nothing into everything with the small lift that some call love.

> *Surmounting the pain of closing and inhabiting*
> *the struggle to open is the daily work of awareness,*
> *from which no one is exempt.*

## Questions to Walk With

- In your journal, describe a time when your anticipation of pain or fear kept you from the whisper of Heaven that was waiting right where you were. Examine this experience as a personal case study and detail what got in the way and what you might do differently next time.

- In conversation with a friend or loved one, describe a time when being held or listened to lessened your fear or quieted your pain. How did this come about? Who can you thank for this? How can you offer the same inner remedies to someone else?

# To Be Radical

The fate of flowers is to blossom
and the fate of human beings
is to grow into our love.

—MN

PEOPLE WHO ARE considered radical are typically associated with advocating complete social or political change. Yet, often, what is first seen as radical is, in time, considered foundational. This brings us to the original sense of the word *radical,* which has a deeper and more compelling notion that comes from the Latin *radicalis,* meaning "inherent, forming the root."

In the plant world, *radical* means "return to the root." And the word *respect* means "to look again." A *radical respect,* therefore, means "to return with open eyes to the root of things." In its deepest sense, to be radical is not veering sharply from the norm but pursuing and returning to the intrinsic nature of things. This speaks to something very essential to being alive.

The great Jewish theologian Abraham Heschel spoke of wonder as a state of *radical amazement* and described this mood of authentic awareness as always waiting below our want to bend everything to our reason:

Standing eye to eye with being as being, we realize that we are able to look at the world with two faculties—with reason and with wonder. Through the first we try to explain or to adapt the world to our concepts, through the second we seek to adapt our minds to the world.

In a similar way, the great Irish poet William Butler Yeats spoke of the moment that we are worn of all ambition into being for being's sake as a form of *radical innocence*:

> Considering that, all hatred driven hence,
> The soul recovers radical innocence,
> And learns at last that it is self-delighting,
> Self-appeasing, self-affrighting,
> And that its own sweet will is Heaven's will.

Far from being rebellious or contrary, the practices of radical respect, radical amazement, and radical innocence are the spiritual covenants of authenticity that keep us connected to each other and the Living Universe.

So, I invite you to be radical in how you walk in the world—with respect, amazement, and innocence. In very personal ways, how do you return with open eyes to the root of things? How do you open your mood of authentic awareness in order to befriend wonder? And how do you work through all you want, to settle into being for being's sake? These are not singular tasks to arrive at but ongoing efforts equivalent to breathing. It is essential to develop these inner skills in order to be fully alive.

What, then, is the root of things that is so fundamental? What is the Larger Order we are returning to? And where do radical respect, amazement, and innocence lead us?

Our place in the world has always depended on our efforts to complete ourselves by finding peace in a sublimely invisible harmony. This is what all the traditions term as mystical: to allow life to unfold beyond what we comprehend.

I admit my bias. I believe in a harmony beyond my understanding of harmony. There's no way to prove what matters; only to say that, when still enough and open enough, we can sense forces at work around us. We live beyond the range of our understanding. Like a stone in mid-fall sensing the gravity that is pulling it closer to the earth. Like a clump of sand sensing the sea that is dispersing it into the tide. Like a lonely heart sensing the power of love that is softening it one experience at a time.

Mysteriously, the larger, more radical order is often out of view. In our journey toward Wholeness, there is a need to withstand the seeming chaos, so we might discover the larger order that is waiting beyond the edge of our knowing.

But being human, we often retreat to what is familiar, rationalizing that the unfamiliar makes no sense, that it is dangerous. When pressed, we tend to fall back on what we are accustomed to, when what is known is just a broken key to a door we can't open by ourselves. And so, we lose our way, three steps from revelation, while it is often those steps that turn chaos into harmony.

The practices of radical respect, radical amazement, and radical innocence help us shed a smaller order for a larger order—until self, other, world, and God are One. Inevitably, we can't do this alone. We need each other to reclaim our roots. It is how God compels us into relationship.

The truth is there is no *they*. What we see across the divide is us. We have created the systems we suffer under and the walls we hide behind. Therefore, to be truly radical is to work with care and respect toward uncovering our common, human roots.

Seeing each other and our conflicts within a larger sense of things has always softened the path. This is one reason the arts are so necessary, because they can throw us back into the larger currents where our self-importance and pain shrink into proper perspective.

One of the leading figures in conflict transformation, John Paul Lederach, speaks of how story, music, and touch have always transported us beyond our familiar frame into the larger currents of Time. He suggests that the power of the arts jars us back into a sense of Oneness that refreshes our approach to each other. This has always been so.

This brings to mind the French philosopher Henri Bergson, who spoke of Time as an ongoing river, always flowing—upstream, before us, and downstream—everywhere at once. Bergson noted that it is *we* who define Time by *our* limitations. Since we can only be at one place along the river at any given moment, we bend and limit Time into smaller portions, more digestible to us. Therefore, we claim, self-centeredly, that wherever we are along the river is the present. And upstream from that point, we call the past. And downstream from that point, we call the future. The truth is that the river—like Time and Spirit and Life-Force—is flowing in all places simultaneously. It is we who can't comprehend the Oneness of things for very long.

This is more than just interesting. For the courage to apprehend the Whole—whether through its face of Time or Spirit or Oneness—greatly affects our living by giving us access to the power and knowledge of the Whole. Seeing Time as one indivisible current enables us to hear the song of that river, which never stops singing the secrets of Oneness. And accessing the secrets of Oneness, by any means (through love or suffering or the arts which marry both), is part of the promise of the inner world.

In the Native American tradition, time is perceived as a pond in which all instances of life ripple out and into each other constantly, the way rain creates many ripples at once.

In many ways, how we relate to Time and Oneness allows us to return with open eyes to the root of things. In many ways, our love for each other opens our mood of authentic awareness through which we rediscover wonder. And both enthusiasm and exhaustion help us work through all we want until we finally arrive at being for being's sake.

These inward progressions are part of the human journey going back to prehistoric life. Duane Elgin, author of the 1981 classic *Voluntary Simplicity,* has described humans as "homo sapien sapien, he who knows he knows." This has always been a blessing and a curse. It seems we embark complete, but before long, to make our way, we become more separate as we become more aware. With this, a paradoxical journey begins. Over a lifetime, we struggle at first between being unaware and being conscious. Then, the struggle shifts between being self-conscious (watching ourselves go through life) and staying connected (staying embodied in our living).

While being unaware means being oblivious and insensitive to the flow of life around us, to lose self-consciousness means being so at one with the flow of life that, like the iris or hummingbird or snow monkey resting in the water, we become *the one who knows but who sacredly lives what he knows*. In this way, we adapt our minds to the world and become radical by embodying the life we are given. This is what the act of baptism symbolizes in various traditions: dipping our face in the waters of life and coming up embodied.

The Aramaic word for children, *dawnawhie*, refers to "any embodiment or emanation of potential." This beautifully affirms, once again, that the mystery of wonder and Spirit are with us from birth and are carried in our childlike nature, which we are challenged never to lose.

The work of embodiment begins with being present. It's important to note that the word *responsibility* at its root means "our ability to respond." So, living an embodied life begins with our vow to stay present and to respond to life in all its forms.

Kurt Goldstein, an early twentieth-century physician, observed that illness itself is the *inability* of a person, or any organism, to be responsive. Health resides in being responsive, in being responsible for our presence and actions in the world.

In traditional Chinese medicine, the term *spiritual* is used to describe "anything that is life-giving." So, I invite you to be spiritual in what you seek and radical in how you walk in the world. I encourage you to form your soul like a root, digging down while opening up. I urge you to drink from the intrinsic nature of things. I implore you to inhabit the qualities of respect, amazement, and innocence in your daily life. For to be radical is to grow your roots until you are a conduit for the essence of life.

*To be truly radical is to work with care and respect toward uncovering our common, human roots.*

## Questions to Walk With

- In your journal, describe a time when you were truly radical, involved in forming and deepening roots. How did this experience affect you?
- In conversation with a friend or loved one, describe a time when you tried to adapt or bend the world to your concepts and desires. Then, describe a time when you tried to adapt or bend your mind to the forces of the world. How did each experience affect you?

# From Brokenness to Tenderness

———

Whatever makes living precious
occurs in this one life, and this
life never lasts. It's startling,
sudden as lightning. These hundred
years offer all abundance: Take it!
What more could you make of yourself?

—T'ao Ch'ien

THIS SECTION EXPLORES the resources that will help us:

- learn how to endure the storms we encounter, and how to process our grief at what has been lost to these storms, while repairing what can be repaired once the storms have gone.
- and how to create the interpersonal and societal lightning rods that can safely release the intensity of the charged regions of our society.

In 1883, Van Gogh sketched a woman with her face in her hands and called it *Sorrowing Woman*. Ever since seeing that sketch, the notion of sorrowing as a natural process has kept working me. After much reflection, I would offer that sorrowing is a process of emptying the buildup of feelings that allows us to renew and return to a Beginner's Heart. In my own life, I can attest that the difference between sorrowing and sorrow is the difference between swimming and sinking. That difference is very real and fragile. When I stop expressing my sorrow, I start to sink. This all points to a larger, natural, and inevitable process of emptying our experience through the thousand moods we're given as humans so we can stay as open and as close to life as possible. This is an intimate practice that each of us has to discover for ourselves. The chapters in this section explore our want to live and love beyond our limitations, the constant challenge to work with what we're given, the work of helping each other through crisis, a profound lesson from songwriter and poet Leonard Cohen, and the added pain we create and spill on others when not facing our suffering.

# Ten Thousand Hands

THE HEART HAS ten thousand hands that want to lift and hold everything, to leave no dream untried. But the life that carries the heart has only two hands. And so, intoxicated with life, we reach for more than we can carry, and meaning well, we promise more than we can ever hope to care for. In this way, we try to live as many lives as possible rather than inhabit the one life we are given.

Feeling this innate cross-purpose, we are seduced by the want to do everything and to go everywhere—though we can't. It was when forced to lie still after a spinal tap during my cancer journey that I discovered that everything and everywhere is holy. It was humbling to realize that I can find God anywhere, if I dare to stop running and be completely where I am.

Romantically and erotically, we are often seduced by the prospect of so many people to experience and fall in love with. But being human, we can't promise ourselves in all directions and be completely where we are. We can only honor one love at a time. When devoted to this deep truism, the mystery of everything reveals itself through the complete love of one thing.

We sorely fail when trying to tend ten thousand things with just two hands. I know. I have tried. But devote the ten thousand hands to the one thing before us, and the care of the heart can empower us with the strength of those who've come before and those yet to be born. Then, we are stronger than we are and more loving than we can imagine. Let the ten thousand hands of the heart enter the two bruised hands we meet the world with and we can embody the love and care of centuries. When reaching for everything, we inevitably fall short of loving anything completely. But through loving one thing or person thoroughly, we can extend our love to everything and everyone we meet.

Reflecting on this led me to retrieve this poem:

### The Ghost and the Symphony

The heart has ten thousand hands.
They want to love everything.
But we have only two.

And so, we hurt each other and break
the world when we insist on carrying
what no one can carry.

This is the ghost of love.

But ask the ten thousand hands
to love one thing at a time and we
can repair the world and release
the sweetness of Eternity.

This is the symphony of life.

When desperate not to miss anything, it is the ghost of love that urges us to embrace everything at once, which is like trying to carry ten cups of tea with two hands—I will inevitably spill them and burn you. But carrying two cups of tea with the care of the ten thousand hands will make me a conduit for all the tea ever poured, releasing Eternity through one moment of complete care.

When we can accept that everything that matters is near, it is the symphony of life that plays *us* till we can receive everything through the one thing before us. Then, the one sip from the one cup is the elixir we've been waiting for. Once we stop chasing the dream, it is a courage of heart that enables us to inhabit the dream wherever we are.

Serving the ten thousand hands fuels desire, which is the want to experience everything. This stirs us to reject where we are. In truth, the aberration of wanting everything is the life of addiction. In this state, what two hands can hold is never enough, and we are driven to seek more and more and more.

However, a devotion to bring the ten thousand hands into the two hands we have is the essence of longing. This stirs us to *enter* where we are. In this state, longing centers on the need to *release* everything that waits in the experience before us. While desire seeks worthiness outside of us, longing seeks Wholeness inside of us.

Still, we can be drawn to the extremes of reaching for everything or being stuck where we are. When we give ourselves completely to the reach of the ten thousand hands, we can become so intoxicated with the Infinite that we are drawn to be romantic, idealistic, and transcendent, ignoring the very real limitations of life on Earth. Yet when we sink into the difficulties of being human, we can become burdened with the frustrations of our limitations and become pessimistic and defeated, thinking nothing is possible beyond our drudgery. The ongoing challenge for each of us is to stay open to the vitality of life-force that precedes us and outlasts us, so we can become skillful in bringing that endless vitality into the two hands we have, concentrating the power of life—through us—into the very particular gestures of care that are before us.

The Roman philosopher Plotinus said, "Virtue is our tendency toward Unity." This tendency to know, feel, and inhabit everything that is larger than us can only inform us through our commitment to give our all to whatever is before us. When we can bring everything to bear on the moment we are in, the heart opens as a conduit between our one small life and the stream of Oneness that sustains us.

One form of heartwork—of being a spirit in the world—is to make a covenant with the practice of staying true and real, which helps us stay in longing and not desire. The ongoing challenge for each of us is not to chase everything but to bring everything through us to illuminate and release the miracle of where we are. This is the sacred work that ennobles us to come alive and, in turn, to enliven the world.

> *The mystery of everything reveals itself*
> *through the complete love of one thing.*

## Questions to Walk With

- Describe a time when you found yourself reaching with your ten thousand hands, wanting more than one person can hold or experience. What did such desire do to you? Where did such wanting lead you?
- In conversation with a friend or loved one, describe a time when you found yourself giving your all through the two hands you have. What did such commitment do to you? Where did such a commitment of care lead you?

# Working with What We're Given

It felt strange to teach again after my surgery, as if I'd made it through some deep trial and surfaced from a cave. And there were young minds waiting in the light, as if they'd been waiting there all along. Not very far into our first session, a bright thin one, teetering on the edge of all he'd taken in and organized in his short unexpected life, blurted out, "Alright, so you almost bought it. What's the point?"

He was poised, ready to jot down my wisdom. I said, "I don't know." He dropped his pen, exasperated. I went to him, "I'm sorry. I do know." He picked up his pen. I said, "In here," I touched his chest, "the heart knows all. In here," I touched my own, "the heart has eyes." He was scribbling. I put down his pen. "Up here," I tapped his head, "the mind never rests, trying to earn what the soul assumes." He stared at me. I patted him on the shoulder. "You see," I touched my heart, "I do know," then tapped my head, "but I don't."

That conversation happened in my thirties and led me to explore the difference between being broken open and being broken. After many years, I confess, it is still impossible to know why some of us are broken open when some of us are just broken. If we knew how to invoke the difference, we could change the course of history. Even within one life, we can experience transformative moments of being broken open and, at other times, we just suffer.

Rather than staying in the unanswerable tangle of why we sometimes evolve and sometimes remain stuck, it is more important to move from one to the other. When broken open, we grow. When just broken, we endure. And the crucial calling of all relationship is to inhabit what we learn from being broken open to help us endure the times we are just broken.

Essential to the practice of compassion is that, when broken open, we find a way to help those who are broken. Equally important is to be humble enough when broken to ask for the help of those who are broken open. In this interdependent way, the light of kindness fills the hole of every pain. We must resist the trial of fairness and the comparison of suffering and devote ourselves to completing each other as we tumble through time. Compassion, it seems, arises when the heart accepts that, regardless of the obstacle or issue, there's nowhere to go.

And when facing the obstacle before us, our ongoing practice is to realize what we're doing or not doing. This is the work of self-awareness. Once our action or inaction is clear, then we can concentrate on putting a stop to whatever behavior is disheartening and draining. This is the work of being. After we see clearly and stop what is life-draining, we can finally course-correct, which is the heartwork necessary to stay real.

But things like fear get in the way. I'm coming to see that when afraid, we take more than we need. Yet when we can accept that love is the sea we move through, we give more freely. For no fish owns the water it swims through, though it can't live without it. And no bird owns the sky it glides through, though it can't fly without it. And none of us own the care that builds within us. If we keep it to ourselves, we drown. It only brings us alive when we give it away.

I recently awoke with an image that goes back to my youth, when sailing on the thirty-foot ketch my father built in our backyard. I spent many summers crisscrossing the Great South Bay off Long Island. When sailing close-hauled in a fierce wind, the boat would lean so far over that the leeward rail would submerge in the water. It was exhilarating and at times dangerous. The remedy when leaning too far was to sail more directly into the wind. This would allow the sails to spill the force of the wind and, in an instant, the boat would right itself and the sails would simply flutter.

This offers a lesson in how to cope with fear and urgency and desperation. While fear, if listened to, will have us lean over and look away, there is a deeper law of human nature that urges us to turn directly toward the force of what we fear. For this will allow our mind and heart to spill the force of what we fear. Facing what we fear directly will allow us to right ourselves. Of course, it takes a steady form of courage to face what we fear, which, if faithful to, will turn into a practice that restores our equilibrium.

Over time, it's clear that the things we suffer and the things we love provide us with an inner curriculum, all in service of working with what we're given while staying close to what we love. Some of the things I have been drawn to learn and explore with others include:

- awakening to the paradox and true gifts of suffering,
- seeing obstacles as teachers,
- letting the life of poetry and the poetry of life continue to blur,
- understanding creativity as an expressive form of healing,
- surrendering the want to be great for the great chance to be,
- understanding how giving attention is more essential than getting attention,
- awakening to the acceptance of our limitations,
- and awakening to how we need each other to be complete and useful.

To learn from all these efforts, we need a deep patience because we can't see around corners. Because life is a perpetual storm, a turbulence of light and dark that coils around each quiet center that we call a soul. We need such patience, not just to endure the turbulence, but to stay close to our full humanity, in order to access the quiet center of our soul, which is where our lasting strength resides.

About twenty years ago, I witnessed a telling conversation about patience with Joel Elkes, a legendary psychiatrist and painter who was a child of the Holocaust. Joel and I were deep friends. At the time, Joel was ninety-three. He was speaking to a handful of college students, unfolding the story of his long life and his journey through World War II. He was remembering his father, Elkhanan Elkes, and the last Rosh Hashanah in the Kovno Ghetto in Lithuania under Nazi occupation. There was a hush in the room. Afterward, one of the students approached Joel with his heart in this throat and asked, "Dr. Elkes, after all you've seen, what would you say is the greatest human strength?" Joel leaned his chin on his cane while sitting and stared across the century and said, "To wait and endure."

It is from the ground of such waiting that our faith in life deepens and widens. No one is exempt from the turbulence of life but we all have access to the peace from which the storm arises and the peace to which the storm, once spent, returns. This is hard to remember when in the storm. But though the surf may throw me under, I still believe in the sea.

And while we can't anticipate life's challenges, we can prepare our fortitude, the way Olympic athletes train. There is a difference between being physically hurt or wounded and being sore from exercise or hard work. So, it's important to make a distinction between heartache and heart-soreness. Heartache comes from living life and being broken open, while being heart-sore comes from the healthy use and exercise of the heart when loving, working, or being in the world. Just as our arms and legs will be sore from exercise to build our strength and stamina, our heart will also be sore from the inner work of loving, working, and caring. These ongoing efforts will build our inner fortitude.

In Japan and China, there is a resilient and delicate tradition of silk-screen painting. Early on, it was discovered that both fine silk and rice paper absorb ink the way a paper towel does. Except where a paper towel tears, the silk and rice paper, both porous and strong, reveal unexpected patterns which preserve the strokes that touch them. This serves as a remarkable metaphor for the mature heart, which doesn't tear when touched, but rather absorbs, reveals, and preserves the essence of what touches it.

Over a lifetime, the strength of an open heart is very much like an ink painting on silk whose landscape reveals the trail of all that we have loved and lost along the way. If I could, I'd open my chest and show you the beautiful, intricate silk screen of my heart. But since we can't, we are left with the endless hours of honest conversation with which to show each other all that has touched us.

I invite you, then, to go inward to the place where you can see the silk painting that is your heart. Some call this journey inward introspection. Some call this the journey of meditation. Some call this the quiet dialogue between self and soul. Let's call it that for now.

So, take your time and look inside, without any purpose, until you start to see the heart-center from which you know the world. Look through the turbulence that surrounds you until the heart of where you've been starts to show itself. Once there, note the intricate landscape stroked on the silk of your heart and revisit the stories of how each stroke came to leave its mark.

By working with what we're given, our soul shows itself. And between what we want and let go of, there rises a difference we could call music. Hearing this difference lets us know truth, which like a note of rain can soften us in an instant. Though mastering the instrument that is our heart can take a lifetime.

*The things we suffer and the things we love*
*provide us with an inner curriculum.*

## Questions to Walk With

- In your journal, tell the story of a time when your ability to be patient helped you endure a difficult time. What did waiting reveal to you that urgency did not?

- In conversation with a friend or loved one, discuss one time when you were broken open and what was opened in you. Compare this to a time when you felt just broken. How did these difficult experiences shape who you are?

# The Suffering in Not Suffering

Maybe the ancient Cynics
were correct—

a thing never quite
appears until it flutters
from the throat—

—Robert Mason

In dodging the lot of being human, we become desperate in trying to avoid the pain of our experience. This leads to unconscious suffering, pain that we feel sharply though we can't quite locate it. And so, we swat blindly at ourselves and others, in attempts to alleviate the acuteness of our suffering. There are a variety of ways that we tend to do this.

## Avoiding Our Vulnerability

If our woundedness is not treated with love and truth, it can lead to these painfully hidden misunderstandings: that the only way to be heard and valued is to be negative, critical, or destructive ("The squeaky wheel gets the oil"), and that the only way to be safe and free is to remain invisible (because the world is always out to get you or use you).

But the opposite assumptions are basic to our sense of aliveness: the most enduring way to be heard and valued is to be who you are, for being who you are naturally leads to appreciation, reverence, and creativity (the rewards of authentic relationship), and the safest and freest place is to live in the open.

In time, we are asked to tend to our vulnerability as we would the iron hub of a wheel on a cart that carries all we own. If not cared for, the hub will rust and the wheel will crumble. If oiled and kept clean, it will carry us everywhere without a squeak. But if we dwell in our woundedness, removed from love and truth, we tend to dig in and retaliate rather than dig down and plant.

## Living Under the Reign of Ego Dominance

There is a children's story that carries the stark isolation and strain of worthlessness that oppresses us when living at the mercy of a fear-driven ego. I'm referring to the modern classic *The Wizard of Oz*. If we look at the story and its array of characters as aspects of a single self, we begin to see a profound dynamic at work.

The wizard is working fearfully behind his screen, darkly manipulating everyone else to protect himself from the pain of living. He is afraid to show himself and afraid to confront the wicked witch, or the good witch for that matter. He is afraid to show himself at all in the world. He holds the Scarecrow, the Tin Man, and the Lion, as well as Dorothy, hostage; bartering what they need to be complete and whole in exchange for slaying what he is afraid of.

All the while, the frightened man behind the curtain maintains his inflated persona as a powerful wizard, when he is, in fact, bankrupt of any authenticity. When the wizard hesitates to fulfill his promises, Dorothy's dog, Toto, pulls back the curtain, exposing the wizard as a con man operating machinery. He resembles Professor Marvel, the fortune-teller Dorothy met back in Kansas. Of course, we are delighted, in the end, to learn that the source of brains, heart, courage, and home all live within us.

Consider the web of relationship that the story unfolds. Whether we consider these the dynamics of a single psyche or of a dysfunctional family, *The Wizard of Oz* portrays a dark, controlling figure who promises worth in exchange for protection. Many family systems work this way, and so, too, do many arrangements of unworthiness within a single person.

This dynamic—of promising worth and affection in exchange for protection—is the workhorse of conditional love. We see it in our quiet partner who wants us to be social for them. And, when not living their own lives, we feel the pain of their demand as they withdraw and turn away from the world. In truth, we are playing wizard and Scarecrow all by ourselves when we barter with the Universe at the well of our confusion, saying, "Please, I will not make any trouble, if you will only tell me that I am safe."

In essence, be it a relentless mother or an insatiable inadequacy within ourselves, we all experience the pain of ego dominance when doing things we don't believe in, in exchange for acceptance or love or the promise of safety or worth.

## Not Meeting Outer Experience with Inner Experience

Once we drift from being who we are, a gap arises in our experiential integrity. The space between our inner life and outer life, between our feelings and our actions, grows and takes on a life all its own. A great deal of our false living gets deeply ingrained when we start putting effort into maintaining this buffered space, rather than maintaining the effort to be congruent. In this way, the frightened man behind the curtain becomes a slave of false living the instant he becomes devoted to living behind his image as a great wizard. He doubles his sufferings when he puts all his energies into not being seen.

This speaks to a dissonance we all know well. How many times have we languished in the corner at a party, listening politely to someone who is shouting softly from behind their mask? How many times have we hidden behind our own verbal screen, wondering if it might be safe enough to come out? Yet, though it is human enough to experience these cautions and lapses in authenticity, we find ourselves in Hell the moment we start to hide from life.

Another story of the modern age that gives us a powerful example of living behind an image is Oscar Wilde's novel *The Picture of Dorian Gray* (1891). Deeply akin to *The Wizard of Oz* in its psychological ore, the story of Dorian Gray shows us, more graphically, the cost of severing our feelings from our actions. For years, Dorian Gray rejoices in the fact that everything he experiences magically happens to his portrait and not to him. In this way, he experiences a sense of immortality, seemingly free of emotional responsibility and free of having to experience his own pain.

In the end, however, in addition to the inevitable pangs of conscience that overwhelm him, Dorian Gray, as his name suggests, finds that, without the depth of having his inner life connected to his outer life, his time on Earth is, in fact, very gray and two-dimensional. Endless years are ultimately worthless, if they cannot be inhabited with honest feeling and connection.

We all suffer the plight of Dorian Gray when we carry around our own little portraits, as image-shields that we put forward; little framed masks that we wear like placards at work, at play, at love; hoping to save ourselves from the emotional responsibility of experiencing our own life. There is no escaping our life and the effort to do so is a Hell all its own. Sooner or later, no matter how well we think we are situated in our facade, the grayness infects our days, and living behind a facade or portrait or even behind a wizard's screen just isn't enough.

## Denying Our Spiritual Needs in Deference to the Expectations of Others

How many times have we secretly feared the pain of being alone so much that we give up aspects of our life in order to be attached? I think this is how I wound up getting married for the first time when I was twenty-two. My wife-to-be came knocking on my lonely door one night and, though I was not ready to fall in love, I succumbed to the comfort of her lightness, rather than accept the pain of my loneliness. In this way, I doomed our time together from the start.

This raises a central and prevalent question. Rather than enduring the discomfort of facing ourselves, how often do we run into the diversion of sex or emotional entanglement? There is an entire strain of recovery work based on this question. Using the same principles as Alcoholics Anonymous, these gatherings are forums for sex and love addicts (SLAA) to confront their compulsions to be with others rather than to face themselves.

The entire program operates on the profound insight that human beings can be as addicted to relationships as they can be to alcohol or drugs. For we can hide in the intoxication of a relationship as easily as that of a drink and use relationships to divert or numb ourselves from the truth of our lives. When the discomfort of authentic living starts to tear through our illusions, we can fall into the comfort of another rather than face our own pain and quandaries in being alive.

With this in mind, let's look at another seemingly innocent fable, the animated Disney classic *The Little Mermaid*. This fairy tale captures the perennial struggle we all face when we deny our spiritual needs in deference to the expectations of others. In this story, the little mermaid, Ariel, so wants to be loved that she gives up her voice in exchange for legs. But giving up who she is to meet the demands of love represents a seductive and tragic want that lives in us all: the want to be rescued from the truth of uncovering and being simply ourselves.

As a story about relationship, the lesson of Ariel is crucial. On the surface, her want for legs seems touching and sweetly motivated by love and the want to belong. Yet, here, too, is another bargain with false living that plagues everyone who ever tries it. For, no matter how badly we want to love or be loved, we cannot give up essential parts of who we are in exchange for love and survive inside, where it counts.

As a story about being in the world, *The Little Mermaid* leaves us with a compelling question: At what cost might we try to have everything? As a mermaid, Ariel is not content to live in the sea. She wants the land, too. Intoxicated with the possibility of life where she is not, she is willing to deform herself to taste it all. Embedded in this is the shadow-side of the American Dream. Yes, anything is possible—go ahead, reach for the stars—but beware of the under-belly of want that never lets where you are be enough.

Of course, there is nothing inherently wrong with change or variety or newness or with improving our condition. The catch is when we are asked to give up our voice in order to have it all; when we are asked to silence what makes us unique in order to be successful.

When not making waves means giving up our chance to dive into the deep, we are bartering our access to God—our deepest chance to belong to the Mystery of Life—for a temporary sense of belonging that may or may not last.

When we give up part of who we are to belong, we empower who we love with the authority to make us whole. No one has that spiritual power. Thus, a sign that we are living in a partial or mitigated relationship is when those that we emotionally depend on keep asking us to suppress or give up aspects of ourselves in exchange for their love. At last, you know you have found a true love when you say, "I would do anything for you," and your other replies, "Would you be yourself?"

## The Denial of Our Kinship to Love, Relationship, and God

When we are busy threading our entanglements and are drawn off-center by the tensions of avoiding and distorting our experience, we can, with hardly an awareness, forget our inborn kinship to Love, Relationship, and God.

Being human, we all move in and out of our deepest connections. This is no cause for shame. For, until you acknowledge falling down, you can never get up. Until I acknowledge that I fall down, too, we can never have a conversation about it. Until we both acknowledge that falling down and getting up is part of being alive, we can never begin to describe the physics of falling down and getting up. But all of this requires admitting our gifts and their mysterious origins, as well as our limitations.

It makes me think of Nicodemus, the one Pharisee who secretly believed in Jesus and who would meet with him anonymously at night to have deep spiritual conversations. But he would never acknowledge his association with Jesus in the light of day. Of course, this did nothing to the essence of Jesus, but traumatically thwarted and plagued Nicodemus for the rest of his days.

This story shows us the quiet pain that comes from not honoring what we know to be true, even if all we know to be true are the questions we are asking. It is even more useful to realize that we each carry a Jesus and a Nicodemus within us: that is, we each have a divine inner voice that opens us to truth and a mediating social voice that is reluctant to show its truth to others.

The British child psychologist D. W. Winnicott called these aspects of personality our True and False Self. Essentially, the True Self is that which lets us know what is real and authentic, while the False Self is that which becomes a diplomat of distrust, enforcing a lifestyle of guardedness, secrecy, and complaint.

In daily terms, our ability to discern what is true or whole from what is false or partial grows from inhabiting the risk to stay real. Often, when we experience a change in reality, we are challenged to bring the way we live into accord with that new sense of truth. In minute ways, we are faced with hundreds of these decisions every day.

## The Practice of Staying Real

I have found that the practice of staying real, like the practice of breathing, is the work of continually making authentic decisions and inhabiting them, so that our gestures in the world stay connected to the voice of our inner being. Yet, very often, we continue, out of habit or fear, to behave in old ways, even though we know that the way of things has changed. Time and again, I have found myself at this crucial juncture: having to admit that what was essential is no longer essential and, then, summoning the courage to make the act of living essential again.

I know that every time I hear or see the truth but hold to the old way—of being, thinking, or relating—I am giving my life over to the

Nicodemus in me. In doing so, I embark on a divided life, in which the divine inner voice can't be ignored, but can't be openly honored.

This is inner embarrassment—catching ourselves in the act of split-living. Yet we can repair in an instant of truth, by letting the God within us show itself out here in the world. However small, this one repeatable act can restore our common and vital sense of being alive.

If any of these conditions speak to you, please don't be discouraged or blame yourself, but rather take comfort that you are not alone. I, for one, can write about these things in such detail, because I've lived out every one of them. So, take comfort in our humanness and devote yourself to the art of making paddles for your canoe, and to mastering the skill in using them.

*No matter how badly we want to love or be loved,*
*we cannot give up essential parts of who we are in*
*exchange for love and survive inside, where it counts.*

## Questions to Walk With

- In your journal, describe a time when you were asked to give up part of who you are in exchange to be loved. How did you meet this challenge? How did this request and your response to it affect your integrity of self and the integrity of the relationship?
- In conversation with a friend or loved one, describe a time when you lived behind a screen like the Wizard of Oz, a time when you pretended to be other than you are. Why did you do this? How demanding was it to keep up the pretense? What led you to come out from behind the screen?

# A Broken Hallelujah

My wife, Susan, and I recently stumbled into the depth of Leonard Cohen's presence and music. We were familiar with his songs and poems, but were being drawn into truly listening to him, into being in conversation with his spirit. Through that listening, we discovered Rufus Wainwright, another original voice. Along the way, Susan found this incredible version of "Hallelujah" written by Leonard Cohen and sung by Rufus Wainwright with an enormous choir of souls. Imagine one man surfacing this song, through the rough channel of his heart, alone in his apartment with his guitar back in the early 1980s. And thirty-two years later (on June 11, 2016), it was sung by fifteen hundred souls in the Hearn Generating Station in Toronto, Canada, five months before Leonard Cohen's death.

Like most artists, Cohen felt a sense of being an instrument through which his deepest songs would rise. While accepting the Spanish Prince of Asturias Award in 2011, the poet-songwriter said, "Poetry comes from a place that no one commands and no one conquers. So I feel somewhat like a charlatan to accept an award for an activity which I do not command."

Indeed, it seems that the song "Hallelujah" commanded him. It originally had eighty verses. It was a voice that wouldn't stop leading him. Cohen once told Bob Dylan that it took him two years to write the song. But no record label would even consider recording the song in its entirety and the mystical songwriter had to choose four verses. The song first appeared as a track on Cohen's album *Various Positions,* originally released in 1984, though Sony Records was hesitant to release the album at all once completed.

Since then, the song has been recorded by artists and choirs worldwide in more than three hundred versions and used as a soundtrack for countless films and TV shows. However, in an effort to make the song more church friendly, several versions have eliminated Cohen's deep and holy tension between being both human and spiritual at the same time. Throughout his long career, Leonard Cohen would often sing a different combination of verses in live concerts.

The word *hallelujah* comes from the Greek meaning "Praise the Lord." The Hebrew version of the word means "Praise God!" From a songwriter and poet as human and all-encompassing as Leonard Cohen, we can understand this command of praise as more than an encouragement to look on the bright side of things.

More deeply, we are required to be fully human in order to face the hardships of living and to *still* praise the larger forces of life that carry us forward anyway. The way the swell and crash of a wave praises the ocean that lifts it. The way a seed in the mud praises the light it cannot see that is drawing it to break ground. The way a broken bone praises the unfolding of time that lets it heal. The way a bird with a broken wing, as the Greek poet George Seferis tells us, praises the wind that allows it to keep flying. When broken, as we all will be at some point in our journey, praising the larger forces of life—singing "Hallelujah"—will help us breach, break ground, heal, and soar, one more time.

The teacher Alisa Ungar-Sargon suggests that "The song's central premise is the value, even the necessity, of praise in the face of confusion, doubt, or dread." That the holy and the broken cannot exist without each other is at the core of being a spirit in a body in time on Earth. Leonard Cohen echoes this perennial wisdom in another song of his, "Anthem," with his famous line, "There is a crack in everything. That's how the light gets in."

We are all clumsy and, under all our awkwardness, graceful, if we can endure the clumsiness. We are all agitated and, under all our tension, at peace, if we can outlast the agitation. And yes, we are all fearful and, under that slow bead of terror that plagues us, no matter its cause, we are ultimately safe beyond our circumstance, if we can breathe under the fear long enough to shed it. If not by ourselves, then with the help of each other.

Yet even when clumsy, agitated, and fearful, we can receive grace through our brokenness as well as our openness. This tension of traversing the human terrain to meet or release what is spiritual is a common theme in Cohen's songs and writings, which bear more than one listening or read-through.

The second verse of "Hallelujah" speaks of the pleasure and suffering that King David experienced for loving Bathsheba. And though the journey between them broke him, she still drew "hallelujah" from his lips. It seems no one is exempt from being humbled by the human journey and no matter how far we fall, no one is precluded from having the light flood through the cracks of our brokenness.

The Jesuit philosopher Pierre Teilhard de Chardin said, "We are not human beings having a spiritual experience, but spiritual beings having a human experience." And yet, I think Leonard Cohen would say, what's the difference? Don't we live in the very center between our pain and the song of life, always being shaped by both? Isn't any path to accepting our frailty and the light we carry equally just and sacred? Ultimately, it doesn't matter whether you rise or fall your way into being fully alive. And most of the time when broken, we are stripped of all that is unnecessary, which only readies us for grace.

The breadth and depth of the song confirms our very flawed existence and the fact that, through our flaws, we are supported by the deeper currents of life, whether we are full of wisdom or dragging around our bag of mistakes.

What Leonard Cohen emphasizes throughout all his work is that neither drowning in our pain nor running from it will let the light in. Only staying broken and open, in the midst of all our flaws, will give us access to the resources beyond us that will sustain us.

In ancient Roman mythology, Janus is the god of beginnings, gates, transitions, doorways, and endings. He is usually depicted as having two faces, one looking to the future and one to the past. Janus presides over the beginning and end of conflict. He is the fulcrum between war and peace, within the individual as well as between nations.

Leonard Cohen's "broken hallelujah" points to two more faces in the life of a soul on Earth: how we are birthed in the breach between pain and song; one face grimacing at all we have to go through, the other in humble awe at the everlasting life-force emanating from the Oneness of the Universe that holds us completely, even in our pain.

Earlier, I mentioned Leonard Cohen's acceptance speech for the Spanish Prince of Asturias Award. In his very moving remarks, he shares how he found the voice inside all his songs. He recalls being a young man, not yet able to play the guitar. He was visiting his mother's house in Montreal. The house was beside a park, and wandering there, he came upon a young Spanish flamenco player strumming in astonishing fluidity across the afternoon. There was a small crowd. Cohen waited till everyone left and asked the young man to give him lessons.

The next day, they began. After hearing Cohen play haltingly, the young Spaniard tuned his student's guitar, but it made little difference. Then, the young Spaniard took the guitar and showed Cohen a sequence of six chords that are at the heart of all flamenco music. But the novice couldn't play them. So, the young Spaniard gently placed his student's fingers on the frets and played the chords with him. And for three days, the young teacher appeared like an angel of music, playing the chords over his student, through his student, with his student.

But on the fourth day, the young teacher didn't come. Concerned, Cohen called the boarding house in another part of Montreal where the Spaniard was staying. Only to learn that the man with the fluid hands had taken his life.

And fifty years later, Leonard Cohen was admitting that all his music has come from those six chords. He never knew why the young Spaniard took his life, but Cohen came away with a deep understanding that we must learn the basic chords under everything. This is the call of every life awakened between its pain and its song. The ordinary heroism of the soul's journey on Earth is to honor and inhabit the comingled origin from which both pain and song arise, so we can play the chords from which all song and poetry come.

In that same acceptance speech in 2011, Cohen pays tribute to the poetry of Federico García Lorca and the power of art:

> Now, you know of my deep association and confraternity with the poet Federico García Lorca. I could say that when I was a young man, an adolescent, and I hungered for a voice, I studied the English poets and I knew their work well, and I copied their styles, but I could not find a voice. It was only when I read, even in translation, the works of Lorca that I understood that there was a voice. It is not that I copied his voice; I would not dare. But he gave me permission to find a voice, to locate a voice; that is, to locate a self, a self that is not fixed, a self that struggles for its own existence. And as I grew older, I understood that instructions came with this voice. What were these instructions? The instructions were never to lament casually. And if one is to express the great inevitable defeat that awaits us all, it must be done within the strict confines of dignity and beauty.

This last sentence of his is deeply profound and bears looking at more closely. The word *express* has three meanings: to give voice to feelings or thoughts, to squeeze out as you might express toothpaste from a tube, and to cause inherent traits to develop as in genetics when a gene for blue eyes will express itself in a child once born. With this in mind, if we are "to express the great inevitable defeat that awaits us all"—death, then how are we to voice the Mystery that gives us life and then takes it away? How are we to squeeze out the dark tangle of fear that accompanies all our thoughts of death? And how are we to inhabit the give and take of life—the smaller births and deaths—that we are born with in our spiritual DNA?

Leonard Cohen suggests that the only way to express the Mystery of Life in all its dimensions is through "the strict confines of dignity and beauty." I think he is referring to the truth of art that arises from the authenticity of our being. The way that canals and sluiceways channel water to where it is needed, dignity and beauty channel the wonder and difficulty of life to where it is needed.

Like all soothsayers, Leonard Cohen was vigilant in showing us the places we can't understand that will not break; though if we fight them, they will break us. For carrying a soul in human form is like being a lamp left out in a storm. Our humanness is the shade that is torn over time and it's only through the rips and breaks in our humanness that the light of our soul shows itself directly. To stay faithful in both directions, inwardly and outwardly, is our broken hallelujah. To do this within the "confines of dignity and beauty" is to be truthful but not indulgent. And to be honest and tender in how we face life is to allow suffering and beauty to mix within our hearts, so that our totality of being can soften the harshness of living.

There is an African proverb that says, "When death finds you, may it find you alive." This anonymous wisdom encourages us not to die while still alive by becoming preoccupied with death. But to stay as fully alive as possible, as long as possible. And it is our sustained relationship with the Universal, while devoting ourselves to the particular, that enlivens the heart to negotiate the hardships we face. For it is a hawk's sustained love affair with the wind while staying devoted to the repeated pump of its wings that enables it to fly.

Ultimately, the notion of "a broken hallelujah" points to something essential that is unnamable, which asks us to live life authentically, devoting ourselves to the full spectrum of the human journey, from tragedy to wonder and back. In deep, immediate ways, the raft crushed at sea doesn't minimize the majesty of the sea or the tragic suffering of whoever is on the raft. We are asked to honor both. To stay devoted to the painful truth of this journey while still honoring the majesty of life is a noble exploration.

And just as the sun is constant, no matter the weather, the Oneness of the Universe is always there, regardless of the clouds of pain, loss, worry, and fear that fog our view. While our experiences under the clouds of living are real, our constant challenge is not to make the clouds our only reality. The courage to face the truth of our experience is necessary, because it is our authenticity that burns off the cloud cover that pain, loss, worry, and fear can generate in our mind and heart.

What is there to do, then, but to live wholeheartedly under both the cloud and the sun, holding nothing back, and loving life and each other anyway? This is how we sing our broken hallelujah, how we live between the pain and song of life, how we vow not to die before we die. So that when death finds us it will pause, the way the creep of night bows its head in wait for the sun to set in its magnificence, day after day. Until we do it all again. Until we can do it no more.

*We must learn the basic chords under everything. This is the call of every life awakened between its pain and its song.*

## Questions to Walk With

- From his Spanish guitar teacher, Leonard Cohen learned the six basic chords of all flamenco music. He later understood that all of his music came from these six chords. In truth, we each must learn the basic chords under everything that help us through life. In your journal, describe what these basic chords are for you; that is, what do you experience as the basic agreements of life under all our trouble that help us find grace through our humanness?
- In conversation with a friend or loved one, name one instance of your own "broken hallelujah," describing a time when you had to face the hardships of living and still felt called to praise the larger forces of life that carry us forward.

# No Greater Teacher

THERE HAS BEEN no greater teacher in my life than the heart. It has guided me through every storm. When facing death, it steadied me despite my fear. When stumbling in need of love, it opened me like a flower waiting for rain. When freefalling in search of meaning, it picked me up like a hawk gliding on the wind of Mystery. And when in need of strength to keep believing in life, my heart insisted that I keep giving as an act of mitosis in growing the tissue of humanity. And so, I'm compelled to explore the heart as our teacher and how we are led to discover and inhabit our need to love and learn and be.

This steadfast belief in the properties of the heart go back to my first hours on Earth. In late February of 1951, I was born premature, three weeks early. I was placed in an incubator and so, I entered a transitional period of solitude before entering the world. This period of incubation prevented my mother and father from holding me and from bringing me home. I'm sure that was difficult for them. But during this crucial time, I was held and nurtured by the Mystical Unity of Life. For those three weeks, I was in a liminal womb, where I went from forming inside my mother to imprinting my deeper senses to the Whole of Life. And this became my primary inheritance.

As I was held and tended by nurses who I will never be able to thank, I quietly continued to form into a full human being. During this slow arrival into the world, I began to inhabit a deep and early sense of Oneness. Being completely alone in that incubator enabled me to experience the solitude and silence of an inner unfolding that was my first home. And though I felt a myriad of volatile emotions from growing up in an unpredictable and emotionally charged family, that turbulence didn't define me. For I could always enter silence and return to my larger, first home.

Looking back, I feel certain that this unexpected cocoon between worlds secured my bond with Eternity. That chance to be fully alone, suspended between pre-life and life itself, allowed me to emerge with an irrevocable bond to all that remains unseen. It allowed me to know all that is unseeable as my foundation. And so, from the outset, the allegiance of my heart has always been to serve as a conduit between all that is inner and all that is outer, between the life of the soul and the life of the world, and between our humanness and the Web of Mystery that brings life into being.

In truth, regardless of where life has led me, my education as a student of the heart traces back to this fundamental position in life. And living through my heart has always helped me through the storms of life and brought me home. This is why I believe that helping each other return to our largest home of all, life, is an essential form of hospitality. This is why I believe that holding and tending each other, as we form inwardly, is at the center of unconditional love. This is why I believe that being at home in the Oneness of Things is central to how we come to love and learn and be.

After all these years, I've come to see that the heart is meant to follow light and connect with life, the way a flower seeds in the dark, breaks ground after a storm, and opens in the light. Once rooted in the open, we are asked to practice heaven.

How the heart teaches us to do this is a lifelong journey. It is interesting that the word *journey* comes from the Old French *jornee,* which means "a day's travel, a day's work." It is still true that a meaningful journey is built on a day's travel and a day's work. And so, the rest of this book tries to describe the heart's process of daily travel and daily work in as much detail as possible, the way that Lewis and Clark described their unlikely passage through the Continental Divide to the Pacific coast.

Along the way, I have seen how solitude, silence, and inner unfolding are our home, and I keep trying to discern what covenants and practices enable us to experience these inner elements as teachers. Clearly, we discover as we go and, from the beginning, we are called to live through our heart. But what does this mean and how do we inhabit this as a sacred life-giving practice?

We all must face the archetypal process of clearing out the buildup of patterns and feelings that we accrue from living. This, in turn, allows us to return to a beginner's heart and to re-establish the allegiance of heart by which we can individuate to the point where we can, paradoxically, let other life in. These twin efforts are necessary, if we are to truly live—to be who we are and to let others in.

Once letting life in fully, how can we then serve as a conduit between all that is inner and all that is outer, between the life of the soul and the life of the world, and between our humanness and the Web of Mystery that brings life into being? How can we inhabit the ways of heart that will help us survive the storms we face? And what commitments and practices can help us live wholeheartedly in the larger flow of life?

To be thoroughly alive, we must look to the learning ground of intimacy, that experiential bedrock of truth where all learning takes up residence in us, when we dare to hold and tend each other.

Ultimately, there are infinite ways for us to personalize our heartwork in the days that await us, if we can empty our assumptions and conclusions in order to stay current to the rush of life. All so that the heart can carry what matters. Yet humbly, no one quite knows how to empty what is extraneous and how to carry what matters, though do it we must. And so, we must live into the question: How do we recover what matters when in the storm? For every spirit must learn its own practice of return to our largest home of all—life. And our quiet destiny is to practice this hospitality in all directions and to let the heart be our teacher.

*Living through my heart has always helped me*
*through the storms of life and brought me home.*

## Questions to Walk With ═══════════════════

- In your journal, describe your deepest home.
- In conversation with a friend or loved one, tell the story of a time when your heart was your teacher. How did it present itself? How did you realize it was a teacher? What did it teach you?

# Heartwork

Don't be ashamed to be a human being, be proud! Inside you, one vault after another opens endlessly. You'll never be complete, and that's as it should be.

—Tomas Tranströmer

We are engaged in heartwork every second of every day. And the more we accept the heart as our teacher, the more we transform into fully realized human beings.

Consider that the organ we call the heart is the center of our physical existence. Whether awake or asleep, all the blood we have moves in and out of the physical heart to keep us alive through the magical process of circulation. Likewise, the emotional heart is the mystical center of our spiritual existence. And whether clear or confused, life-force moves in and out of the heart we feel with to keep us alive through the magical process of relationship.

As we negotiate the outer world of circumstance, our inner health depends on bringing what is in, out. Consider how all musical instruments are hollowed in order to release their music. And though instruments are hollowed out differently, the emptiness revealed is the same. In this way, each of us is shaped uniquely by experience into a distinct self. Yet we are all hollowed out by life to reveal the same emptiness through which the one Eternal song of life comes into the world.

In this way, each person's heart is an instrument which takes a lifetime to learn how to play. By meeting our experience and being who we are, we discover our scales and chords and bring our song into the world.

It helps to remember that whether plucked, stroked, tapped, bowed, or brought alive by breath, each musical instrument brings song after song out of its hollows into the world. We call this bringing out of the hollows—music. In the same way, we are plucked, stroked, tapped, bowed, and brought alive by breath in our tug of war with experience. This is how the life of experience brings us into the world. We call this continual expression of life out of our hollows—the music of life as played through the heart.

More deeply, heartwork demands that life keeps moving through us. As an instrument serves its purpose when music flows from it, a soul serves its purpose when care flows from it. As fire needs wood, the soul needs care to burn strong and bright. Just as it doesn't matter what kind of wood is given to a fire, the soul doesn't value one form of care over another. Any act of care will make the soul come alive through us. And since all things are worthy of care and in need of care, any ground of experience we devote ourselves to will brighten our aliveness—in us and between us. Simply and profoundly, as a fire needs wood, the soul needs care to thrive.

From an eternal perspective, every life within every generation struggles between the heartache of nothing and the wonder of everything. When hurt and unable to explain pain and loss, we are tempted to make a god of nothing, banishing all that is connective about life. Similarly, when touched by kindness and lifted by inexplicable grace, we are tempted to make a god of everything, wanting to exile the inevitable difficulties of being alive. But the tides of life are always replete with both nothing and everything, as they mix within us and between us. For the Unitive Mystery of Life authors, braids, and sustains the heartache of nothing and the wonder of everything in its indestructible tapestry. And so, we have to accept, honor, and learn from both.

This dance between nothing and everything is one of the chief art forms of the heart. And I confess, after all these years, that while I am willing to prepare for a world of unpredictable difficulty, I am not willing to prepare for a world without miracle. Though I can't explain why, I believe that the pains of living and the ease of being are endless threads in the fabric of life that weave the enduring aspects of existence into our soul—through our heartwork.

In everyday terms, we are challenged to be who we are everywhere by being both strong and vulnerable. In time, integrity is the want to feel everything and become nothing, the want to let everything in while staying true to our own nature. If blessed, we can help each other stay committed to the endless rigor of heartwork. This alone will let us experience more and more of the endless flow of life.

> As a fire needs wood, the soul needs
> care to burn strong and bright.

## Questions to Walk With

- In your journal, describe the instrument that life has shaped you into and the music that comes from you out of the hollows.
- In conversation with a friend or loved one, discuss a time when you felt the press of nothing and how that affected you. Then discuss a time when you felt the lift of everything and how that affected you. Describe your heartwork in dancing between the two.

# A Thousand Stitches till Dawn

———

Until we extend our circle of compassion to all living things, we ourselves will not find peace.

—Albert Schweitzer

THIS SECTION EXPLORES the resources that will help us:

- discover and become skilled at rituals and practices designed to clear the confusion and disorder that live within us and around us.

Aristotle said, "We should never teach a virtue in isolation." And so, to live fully in all directions requires the hard work of listening through the doorway of experience into the realm of all views until we make a tapestry of everyone's experience. The endless practice of bringing all we are not into all that we are is how we stitch the world together repeatedly. This is how we meet the days without hiding our truth or pain, and most importantly, our love. In living through our heart, we reach through the authentic in order to reveal the common web of life that sustains us all. The chapters in this section explore how modern life has split our basic nature, how we are nonetheless challenged to grow our compassion, how we are ever instructed by the paradox of limitation, and how we are one step away from dropping all that weighs us down.

# Secret Identities

THE IMPORT OF ancient mythology, the basis of its gods, was to provide us with larger-than-life figures who could serve as conduits, connectors between us and the elements of the Universe. Apollo, Neptune, and Thor were guardians of the sun, the sea, and thunder. They served as intermediaries between us and the great Unity that exists beyond our limited and partial understanding of the life we move through.

But if we look at our contemporary mythology, as manifest in the modern lore of horror movies, comic books, and reality television, there is a distinct shift in our assumptions as a culture. In place of the ancient impulse to join with other life and be made whole, we find modern stories that emphasize the split and the hidden, stories that mirror our struggles with being fragmented and divided, as well as stories that glorify the secret and the hidden.

In European folklore, the story of the werewolf first appears in the Middle Ages. The very concept of a werewolf reflects our want to divide the innate spectrum of human emotion into desirable and undesirable traits. It implies that any of the more volatile human moods—anger, passion, and aggression—should be denied and suppressed. But denying our more difficult moods rather than facing them only deepens the split in our personality. Such a split only makes the denied aspects of our personality larger and more potent.

In this regard, the werewolf represents the non-integrated human being, and his very lack of integration makes these difficult emotions even more volatile. The only action that can stop the werewolf is the presence of a cross. Yet the cross is not offered as a healing force but as a shaming force.

Hold up a cross and the wolf in us is shamed and rushed into exile—not healed but cast out. Here, we begin to shun part of our human nature. Here, we cease to even desire Unity. And so, hiddenness infects our consciousness rather quickly as a prerequisite of modern existence.

This legacy is deepened in the classic story of Jekyll and Hyde, where a doctor of eminence is doomed to an uncontrollable transformation into a being of pure rage—repeatedly. As early as 1886, this story indicates that we as citizens had become two-faced, keeping up a proper, though unrealistic, public image while hiding our deeper impulses till they inevitably explode.

The comic hero the Hulk is the same conflicted man, recast with our century's doubt about technology, as this hero's transformation into a behemoth of rage is triggered by a technological accident. The sheer existence of these myths is unconscious evidence that we are terribly divided as individuals from the Whole of Life. Suppression by itself is ever more painful the longer these aspects of our nature are subdued, the way an infection worsens if untreated.

Having resigned ourselves to being split and hidden, our contemporary mythology, especially in the form of comic book heroes, has given rise to the secret identity—no longer warning us where our lack of integration can lead, but now sanctioning our inner divisions to the point of glorifying a double life.

These myths take on a telling significance as manifestations of our modern psyche. We keep exhibiting deeper and deeper patterns of escalating estrangement. The more we separate from our inner nature, the more we hide, and the more we hide, the more dangerous the exiled wolf becomes, and likewise, the more idealized and fantasized its opposite, portrayed as a superhero.

Nowhere is this more evident than in the myth of Superman, who is perfect and godlike in all external aspect, but is meek, mild, and hidden as Clark Kent. Interestingly, here, the werewolf's dangerous qualities of anger, passion, and aggression have been transposed into the idealized qualities of justice, action, and service in the character of Superman, while the feminine qualities of receptiveness and tenderness (cast here as being meek and mild) have now become part of his secret identity, Clark Kent.

Our want to be whole, though, no matter how denied, is so powerful that it infiltrates the very myth that spurns it. What replaces the cross that weakens the werewolf is kryptonite, a piece of the planet where Superman was born. In its presence, he becomes less extreme, less godlike, and more ordinary, more fully human, more integrated with his secret identity.

What kryptonite represents is a piece of our origin, our ground, our innate and whole beginning, a piece of where we come from, where, despite the fantasy of unlimited power, we secretly want to return—a source we are so divorced from that it seems like another planet. Kryptonite represents the painful opportunity to give up our fantasies and reintegrate all our traits in order to be real which, in turn, will make us whole and wonderfully ordinary.

This modern myth mirrors how we, in effect, have become a society of spiritual Clark Kents, of individuals aspiring to live out super-dreams—to be super-gods, to accumulate super-wealth, to have super-sex, to go on super-vacations, to be a super-dad, a super-mom, a super-athlete, a super-student, a superstar—while maintaining our less-perfect, more human, secret identity. And what is split and hidden bursts at the seams till there are countless incidents: of public officials who are Jekyll and Hyde, of baseball stars who beat their wives, of religious leaders who are caught in sex scandals, of ordinary lives striving to be perfect in every external aspect while the wolf in exile hungers through the night.

Don't we all maintain a secret identity when we hide what we know? Isn't the largest closet population of all, the closet-aware, those who pretend to know less than they do? And the danger in staying hidden is not being found out, but forgetting that the part that we hide is real.

We are complex beings seeking to be simple and the stories we perpetuate evolve as psychic mirrors of our culture's soul and its struggle with emptiness. The myth of Superman at once shapes our want for the ideal while providing the one element of origin that can bring us back to Earth. So, I must ask: What is your kryptonite? What deep piece of origin will break the strength of your fantasies and make you blessedly ordinary?

There is one mythic story that tries to bridge the split in us. It is the French fairy tale "Beauty and the Beast," where the beast in us, against all suppressed horror, is capable of being loved by what is beautiful in us. In the end, the beast is killed while trying to protect beauty, a sign that what is rejected and shunned in us will, given the chance, love and be loved to the point of putting its volatility to rest.

In more recent times, this story is recast as King Kong, where the beauty in us is more hysterical and resistant, more frightened of the enormity of the beast and more confused by its own attraction toward such a distorted inner element. With this telling, the story re-integrates our idealized virtues with our buried passions. But here, too, the beast in us gives its all to protect and even die for the beauty in us. And the struggle inherent in both versions of this story is still alive, still evolving, still told, still fulfilling some cultural need for Unity and Wholeness.

In the modern world of toys, we find a synthetic totem of our tensions between hiding and joining. I'm referring to Teenage Mutant Ninja Turtles, small plastic warrior dolls who are named after Renaissance figures such as Michelangelo, Leonardo, and Raphael. The cluster of connotations is staggering. *Ninja* represents an expert in ninjutsu, the traditional Japanese art of stealth, camouflage, and sabotage. *Mutant,* in biology, refers to an individual or organism that is monstrously atypical, differing from its parent organism dramatically. A turtle is legendary in its need for a massive shell and known for its ability to swim to vast depths. And the Renaissance is well-known as a great period of cultural rebirth. Talk about mixed messages. We are giving our children play-heroes who are trained in violence and sabotage, who are monstrously different from any parent, who live in a massive shell, yet who can swim to vast depths, and who harken to a time of rebirth. God knows what an innocent mind will make of all this.

As adults, we only have to look to television for the brand of hero we metaphorically emulate: undercover cops, who again glorify the secret identity, and, most revealing, private investigators. Our need to be rescued privately by investigation is so urgent, constant, and deep that we project that inner need onto small mythic heroes who expose the hidden (thieves, murderers, and adulterers) and rejoin the split (kidnap victims, runaways, and hostages)—all in the streets we are frightened to walk.

But the most interesting symbol of our inner conflict stems from an older legend—that of the vampire which at once presents us with a remedy to our separateness while making the solution horrific, violent, and forbidden. A vampire needs to drink the blood of others to survive and those he drinks from, in turn, must do the same. Portrayals of this have been frightening and cannibalistic while recently being recast as seductive and sexual, heightening even further our attraction to and repulsion by such a thing.

Yet, if we strip the violence from all this, we are left with the deep and ancient image of drinking from another's source. There is no more direct way of joining. Boys and men for centuries have become blood brothers as an ultimate symbolic bond. Taken further, this image is at the core of Christian communion, where the devout are asked to symbolically drink the blood of Christ.

In our daily struggle to be real and whole, we are all private investigators, seeking out the source in everything, that we may drink from it and no longer feel the need to stay hidden. All with the hope that we can put down our secrets and our masks and simply be who we are everywhere.

*The danger in staying hidden is not being found out,*
*but forgetting that the part that we hide is real.*

## Questions to Walk With

- In your journal, describe a time when you felt the need to hide some aspect of who you are. Why was this necessary? What was the cost of hiding who you are? How did you remedy this situation?
- In conversation with a friend or loved one, describe someone you know who is completely who they are everywhere. What do you admire about this person? What can you learn from them?

# The Sovereignty of the Seer

THROUGHOUT HISTORY, THINKERS have projected their best thoughts onto our spectrum of human behavior, each of us overlaying another philosophy onto the world. Yet, we are forever reminded that our view is not the only view. Each name for the spectrum of human behavior, each philosophy trying to explain the world, is just one particular view. As is mine.

Still, in my view, four elements of living seem enduring: the individual soul of a life, the communal web of lives, the dynamic flow of the Universe, and the river of experience, that kinetic flash of current that connects them all. Every active mind, literate or not, civilized or primal, has made a god of these elements. They seem the spiritual equivalents of earth, fire, water, and air.

Consider the Jewish philosopher Martin Buber, who said:

> The primary connection of [the human] with the world is comprised in *experiencing,* which continually reconstitutes the world, and *using,* which leads [to] . . . the sustaining, relieving, and equipping of human life.

Buber describes our necessary reliance on the Whole, which, in turn, causes us as parts to live and grow. A person gathers wood from nature and stokes a fire and the experience warms us, which enables us to live and keep the fire going.

Buber leads quite naturally to the legendary Chinese thinker Confucius, who said:

> To find the central clue to our moral being which unites us to the Universal Order [Chung-Yung], that indeed is the highest human attainment.

It is interesting that in the Chinese expression for Universal Order, *Chung* means "central" and *Yung* means "constant." Thus, the highest human attainment is to find and sustain those elements within and without that are central and constant. The assumption is that uncovering and enlisting these elements will cause us to be linked with what has been central and constant in the Universe since the beginning of time. And in spiritual, mental, and emotional ways, the movement of one's life in rhythm with what is central and constant provides an enduring sensitivity and strength. While Buber outlines the nature of survival, Confucius outlines the nature of integral living.

Each of us needs to both survive and live integrally. Therefore, any effort that can bring us to a unified grace between who we are and our being, our community, and the Universe is an integral state of living. Any such effort is a deep and invaluable tool in the practice of life. If the effort shows up as a unifying thought, we can think the thought over and over, until the roots of our mind deepen. If the effort shows up as a way of digging in the earth, we can plant seeds over and over, until things grow where we dig. If the effort shows up as our care for others, we can love ourselves together.

The German philosopher Friedrich Nietzsche ran counter to Buber and Confucius when he said:

> As for the rest of life—so called *experience*—who among us is serious enough for that? Or has time enough? When it comes

to such matters, our heart is simply not in it—we don't even
lend our ear. . . . The sad truth is that we remain necessarily
strangers to ourselves.

Nietzsche may well be the anti-Confucius. He is extolled as the
architect of the modern sensibility whose lament is that the individual is just not up to the task of keeping up with the Whole. According
to Nietzsche, we are debris in the storm and owe no allegiance to the
forces that summon us or scatter us. According to the early work of
the German philosopher, our only recourse is to impose our inexo-
rable will.

Obviously, I am not a member of this club, for while I admit that
there are times that we remain strangers to ourselves, I will never
believe that this is necessary. For this marks the oldest quarrel among
seekers: Is our journey about unity or fragmentation; about order or
chaos; about the struggle of creation that transforms us into an uplifting creature like Pegasus, the winged, Divine horse; or the struggle
that isolates us into a sad creature like Sisyphus, the selfish king who
was punished for cheating death?

Though I must admit that the torque of modern society presses
on us all with its techno-industrial isolation. In the metal and plastic
cocoon of modern days, we tend to accept our lot as strangers—to
ourselves, our communities, and the Universe. Without a chance to
renew our basic nature, we are slowly acquiescing to a modern fate
where we are strangers to our own experience. In this way, our global
culture has taken Nietzsche's questions as commandments: no one
among us is serious enough for experience. No one has time enough
for that.

Inundated with endless information, 24/7, from seven hundred
channels, we are overwhelmed in our isolation with data instead of relationships. The political scientist E. E. Schattschneider speaks to this:

The compulsion to know everything is the road to insanity.
People are able to survive in the modern world by learning
to distinguish what they must know from what they do not

need to know. . . . Democracy is like nearly everything else we do; it is a form of collaboration of ignorant people and experts. . . . We could not live in modern society if we did not place confidence daily in a thousand ways in pharmacists, surgeons, pilots, bank clerks, engineers, plumbers, technicians, lawyers, civil servants, accountants, courts, telephone operators, craftsmen and a host of others.

Of course, people did live without these things. So, the pivotal words here are *survive* and *modern.* To survive in a holistic way requires a *passion* for everything. To survive in a modern way requires a *binary mindset,* adroit at flicking yes or no to what is necessary and what is not.

The concept of willful ignorance, then, becomes a modern strategy of survival, which allows for a trust or collusion to exist between ignorance and expertise. Certainly, it is inescapable. I don't need to know how a TV works to watch the news. I don't need to know how a microwave works to cook baked potatoes.

Economists have termed the domain of such willful ignorance "the sovereignty of the consumer." A troubling phrase, which refers to the rights of the buyer; rights which guarantee the power of purchase and ownership over the power of experience and knowledge; rights which ultimately sever the part from the Whole, which make the part superior to the Whole; rights which become insidious if we think of managers owning athletes, or employers owning employees; rights which turn hideous, if we think of slave owners.

But it is equally true that I don't need to know anything about the science of optics in order to see. I don't need to know the physiology of the heart in order to feel. I don't need to know the history of Western thought in order to imagine. And mystics would call this deeper, innate sense of knowing "the sovereignty of the seer," meaning the innate rights of one who sees, who drinks from, who ingests and inhabits; the rights of one who consumes in the original sense of the word, from the Latin *consumere,* "to take in completely."

And so, the real danger of our age, the real press of society that isolates us, which can be seen everywhere, is the erosion of the sovereignty of the seer. It is a condition that permeates the very fabric of our society. For when surrendering to the saturation of information in isolation, we give authority over our lives to the experts and settle into the shell of our ignorance.

It has become the expected behavior of a model citizen, to be obedient and accepting of the nearest expert, whether they are a journalist or a physician or a store clerk deciding the color of our drapes. Curiosity has become intrusive and even offensive. Ignorance is the default position. It will get you into heaven and keep you out of jail. Its inertia has led us to seek experts for how we see ourselves, for how we see God, for how to dress our dead. There are even expert gift services which will choose the right gift for a loved one. The press of experts is so great that anyone who pursues experience for themselves is viewed as abnormal: a pain in the ass, if we inquire too long into how something works; a radical, if we inquire too long into the truth of a government policy; a relentless adolescent, if we inquire too long into the nature of life.

If Wholeness is the reward for the sovereignty of the seer, as both Buber and Confucius suggest, then comfort is the reward for the sovereignty of the consumer, and comfort is the psychic tranquilizer that makes ignorance bliss, that keeps us from being informed by the Whole.

The contradiction between learning and consuming creates a tension in our sense of education. We are traditionally taught to value extensive knowledge, to become learned, to respect those who gather knowledge. But hidden in the strategy of willful ignorance is the want to learn only what is necessary. The discrepancy ensures a gap in our sense of self-worth. We are taught to aspire to be all-knowing, but are overwhelmingly steered to the truncated pragmatism of willful ignorance. And so, we can never live up to what we are taught to value.

Eventually, every part of life is treated with ignorant urgency: *I don't care what it is, just fix it.* This is why many therapeutic relationships fail, because a good therapist, like a good teacher, wants those before them to do the work for themselves, while those in ignorant need simply want to be fixed and provided with what they've decided they don't need to know.

It's a great deal like going blind and being taken care of, efficiently and comfortably, until you expect, or even demand, someone to cook for you, to wash for you, to tell you which movies are funny, which books have meaning, what your lover really looks like, to tell you what's happening in the world.

Soon, you believe it is your right to be taken care of, to be kept informed. But one day, there is a strange sense of truth that reaches you from underneath everything. And you wonder about everything you were ever told. At this point, many of us grow bitter and never trust what others say ever again. But some of us dig in and listen more closely. And some of us, despite the long journey, begin to build a way of living life for ourselves, questioning if we were ever really blind.

*The movement of one's life in rhythm*
*with what is central and constant provides*
*an enduring sensitivity and strength.*

## Questions to Walk With

- In your journal, describe your experience and understanding of what you know to be central and constant.
- In conversation with a friend or a loved one, describe your own experience as a consumer, feeling the right to have aspects of life provided for you, and your own experience as a seer, feeling the need to inhabit life directly as it comes to you. Discuss the difference.

# The Maturing of Compassion

To listen with our heart will change everything,
regardless of what we think.

—MN

LOVING IS THE practice ground for everything. By loving, we awaken
the heart, sending care into the world through our hands. At the same
time, suffering keeps breaking what can be broken until we reach what
is unbreakable. It keeps undoing what can't last until we are standing
on what will last.

These two forces are spiritual equivalents of centrifugal motion,
which tends to move objects away from the center, and centripetal
motion, which tends to move objects toward the center. Love usually
moves us out into the world, while suffering tends to move us toward
the center by grounding us, even against our will. In large measure,
our human journey evolves by how we inhabit and meet these forces.
The insight and wisdom we gain in our journey through love and
suffering is transformational and enduring.

That we are all on this journey, feeling the torque of love and
suffering, opens us to the life of compassion. We cannot truly feel
without feeling for others. Once something is felt, it cannot be unfelt.
Once something is seen, it cannot be unseen. Though we can close
after opening, out of fear, what has been opened inside us can never
be closed.

As the mystical poet Michael Mejia says, "Pain that is not felt becomes blinding." When we deny the impact of suffering on our being, we go blind to the deeper web of life that supports us. And we go blind to the suffering of others. Yet, as the nineteenth-century Romantic poet Shelley says, "There is no unconnected misery."

And so, when we face what we feel, through both love and suffering, we begin our lifelong exploration of the art of feeling for and with others. Early in life, there is an initiation into the practice of compassion through the commonality of our experience with others. If I have suffered a broken heart, then when I witness your heart breaking, I can easily identify with what you're going through. If you've lost your job and come into my life when I am laid off, we can easily meet in our common struggle with adversity. If I've felt betrayed by a friend or loved one and I'm near you when you are betrayed, we can quickly form a bond that will help each other through. This sort of compassion, based on our common experience, is an ongoing apprenticeship that never ends.

But over the years, as I've thinned what builds between my heart and the world, I've come to see that this form of compassion, dear and necessary as it is, leads to a maturing of compassion. Once our heart is opened, the practice of identifying with others leads us to the noble and necessary act of feeling compassion for those that we have no common experience with.

My first jarring experience of this came when I met a man who served as a medic in the Iraq war. Though I tried to put myself in his place, I couldn't fathom his experience. But I felt compelled to stay with him because he needed someone to listen. I remember sitting in a booth at a bar with him and saying, "I can't imagine what you've been through." He slammed his hand on the table and replied, "No! You Can't!" I awkwardly put my hand on his and uttered, "You're right. I can't. But I'm here." And we went on into a realm of honest conversation neither of us had ever had.

In this regard, a great ever-present challenge for each of us is to be present to everyone and to simply and deeply listen—especially when the suffering of others would have us pull away because it frightens us. In the face of such aversion, we are challenged to stay present beyond our own discomfort. As the priest and humanitarian Henri Nouwen affirms, "Compassion means full immersion in the condition of being human."

The maturing of our compassion opens a wild and tender field of relationship in which we honor the experience of others, no matter how different from our own. Not only does this sort of compassion extend our circle of healing, but it knits the larger fabric of humanity. Eventually, we're called to inhabit a twin practice of compassion: maintaining our care for those we have something in common with, and extending our care to those whose experience is completely foreign to us. And every listening with the heart opens us to another teacher. For through our love of others, we learn and relearn to be intimate with all things.

Brian is a tender example of seeing with your heart. He was part of a yearlong group I was journeying with. We were exploring inner work and our place in the world. During our last meeting, I asked everyone what they had learned during the year. Brian teared up and said that, no matter how he tried to extract a learning from the past year, he kept returning to his memory of his father tying his skates when he was six. At six-thirty in the morning, in the half-blue of dawn, his father would watch him skate before heading off to work.

For Brian, whose father is now gone, this was more than a memory he chanced upon. It was the earned view from having opened his heart, which, after all these years, let him see through his father's eyes. And so, he felt the depth of his father's love in a way he never imagined. This was what he learned in our time together—how to see through the eyes of compassion. Brian's inner work had pried him open and this enabled him to see and feel the arc of life from then to now. The arc of feeling that surfaced through his love of his father allowed him to re-enter an intimacy with all things.

The teacher and community leader Sally Hare suggests that "The purpose of education is to rid ourselves of the illusion of separation between the individual and the community, [between] the internal and the external." This, too, is the purpose of compassion.

In deep ways, compassion is a concentration of our heart's attention that is powerfully present in all directions, including beyond the realm of just what is human. Musicians offer this concentration of heart when they retrieve and play their music. Gardeners offer this concentration of heart when they seed and tend what they plant. Birders offer this concentration of heart when they sight and marvel at the wonder of birds in flight. And painters offer this concentration of heart when they look into the nature of light and try to render what they see on a canvas.

I know an old painter whose spirit is loved by the light that he paints. When he gives his all to watching the light and all the ways it moves between the ancient homes and the thick-rooted trees, the light shows itself to him a little bit more than the rest of us. This is what seeing with our heart can do. This is what unrestrained love can do. It makes life bend toward all that is loving. This is why those who love us see more of who we are than strangers. This is why artists and poets and biologists and teachers see more in their subjects and students than the rest of us. Because their love coaxes the essence of things more fully into the open. In this, we are all artists. For we each have this capacity to love and, through that love, to draw life closer to us. It doesn't matter what skill or craft or work you engage in to manifest this love. Any endeavor—even carrying water or doing the dishes—can become a form of compassion if animated by love.

> *Through our love of others, we learn and*
> *relearn to be intimate with all things.*

## Questions to Walk With

- In your journal, describe a time when your compassion was stirred for another because you discovered some experience you both had in common. How did opening your heart to this common experience affect you and your relationship with this person?

- In conversation with a friend or loved one, discuss a time when your compassion was stirred for another with whom you had nothing in common. What opened your heart to this person? How did opening your heart to this person add to your life?

# Inner Triage

A great song never sung is a terrible storm building within.

—MN

STRANGE HOW PAIN wakens and sadness puts us to sleep, how, in the privacy of what we feel, we writhe and soar, then dress and order tea as if nothing has happened. It's trying to go on as if nothing has happened that drains us of life. For beneath all forms of moral contrition, the wounds we suffer and perpetrate, if never faced, settle in our bones. They will soften us from the inside out. We are all eaten by what remains unsaid, unfaced, unowned. And knowing we must open our entire being like a shut eye while not doing so—this is the real cause of loneliness.

To break our loneliness, we simply have to risk caring. And understanding is not a requisite for compassion. Only seeing that what's broken is still living.

Recently, my wife, Susan, had carpel tunnal surgery. As I was counting the time in the waiting room, I recalled my own surgeries and was stopped by the miracle of surgery and the gratitude of everyone who has ever been repaired by it. This has stayed with me. And now, I am stopped by the miracle of love and the gratitude of everyone who has ever been repaired by that.

Perhaps this is the core purpose of love: to untangle each other's hearts with the surgery of care, to trust someone enough to let them reach way inside to unknot what we can't see or reach, so we can heal.

Isn't this the purpose of therapy? Isn't this one of the core reasons for trust?

In medical terms, *triage* involves assessing the level of urgency regarding wounds and illnesses to decide what needs to be treated first. The concept comes from the French word *trier,* which means "to separate out." What we are exploring here is a form of inner triage, whereby we determine the urgency of mental, emotional, and spiritual wounds in order to treat the most severe injuries first. By what means do we inwardly separate out that which demands our full immediate attention and that which is a later concern or even a distraction?

Medical educator Aurelia Clunie confirms that

> The first evidence [in history] of a surgical procedure is that of *trephining,* or cutting a small hole in the head. This procedure was practiced as early as 3000 BC and continued through the Middle Ages and even into the Renaissance. The initial purpose of trephining in ancient cultures is unknown, although some hypothesize it may have been used to rid the body of [toxic] spirits. The practice was widespread throughout Europe, Africa, and South America. Evidence of healed skulls suggests some patients survived the procedure. Trephining continued in Ancient Egypt as a method of treating migraines.

For centuries, we have tried to rid the body of toxic spirits and to alleviate pressure in the head. The various forms of meditation are all designed to alleviate pressure in the head. The arts, both creating them and experiencing them, all have the power to alleviate dark clouds that reside in the head. Friendship and care certainly alleviate the pressure of anxiety and loneliness. Meditation, art, friendship, and care all bore small holes in our thinking to restore the freshness of direct living.

The primary question of healing has always been, how do we alleviate suffering for each other? It is said that in the age of shamans, the healer of the tribe would sit with someone drowning in their grief and reach with his third eye, thrusting his care—like an invisible hand—into the dark part of the sad one's heart. After a while, the healer would pull the dark cloud of the mourner's grief out of their body, leaving the loss to knit as naturally as possible into the heart's healthy skin. So, it's not just the head that needs to be alleviated of pressure.

As with physical triage, the first thing to do in healing inner wounds is to stop the bleeding and to ensure that breathing and cognition are stable and working. Inwardly, this is tantamount to restoring safety by separating the sense of trauma from the current moment at hand. What I fear most is often looming in the past or the future. And so, I need to re-inhabit the present, with all its difficulties, in order to open the wound.

Once the inner wound is opened to air, there is the need to bandage it. This involves facing what is ours to face in order to disinfect the injury. Dressing the inner wound so it can begin to heal often involves the reception of our pain by loved ones. In tender and resilient ways, our presence serves as a bandage for each other. To hold ourselves open with the help of loved ones until the dark clouds of pain, fear, and despair dissipate is a form of spiritual triage.

We must never underestimate the power of dark clouds to block us from our inborn nature. In the course of a life, there are many things that get in the way or cloud our view, such as pain. Often, when pain takes hold of us, it clouds our thinking and throws us into a dark tumble.

And just as the glare of the sun can block us from what is lighted because of its sudden brightness, the sudden appearance of pain can darken our view and prevent us from seeing what needs to be repaired. For pain can mask the larger flow of things because of its sudden collapsing quality. In its moment of press, pain is all that we feel and see. Understandably, it is a reflex, when hurt, to focus on the point of hurt. Then, for the moment, the whole world is reduced to the cut or throb or ache of emptiness. We can let in little else.

But while we are collapsed, the majesty and flow of life does not stop. And though our pain seems all encompassing, we must resist rewriting the world in the colors of our pain. For we are always more than our pain and fear and despair.

When my wife came to from her surgery, I was by her side. As she brought the world back into focus, she said that she was thirsty. I brought some water to her lips and we began our slow journey home, where we continue to apprentice in the art of living.

*We are all eaten by what remains*
*unsaid, unfaced, unowned.*

## Questions to Walk With

- In your journal, describe three emotional pains or fears that are currently ailing you. Try to prioritize which needs to be treated first. Then, identify who you can turn to in order to open this wound in the light of day. That is, who can listen this wound into the open with you, so it can begin to heal? Lastly, go to this person and begin the healing.

# The Paradox of Limitation

The highest reward for a person's toil is not what they get
for it, but what they become by it.

—John Ruskin

*Thirty-five years ago, I was forced to lie still after a spinal tap during
my journey with cancer. Ever since, I have been an apprentice in the paradox of limitation. Recently, the learnings I have gathered over the years
have come together like beads on a necklace. And so, this chapter tries to
unravel the many learnings and examples I've come upon.*

We all experience limitations. It is an inescapable part of being human. When faced with a limitation, we are asked to devote ourselves
to that limitation as our teacher and to immerse ourselves in the
journey that unfolds. Here is a constellation of stories to bring this
more in view.

It has been almost ten years since my father died, and I continue
to learn from him. There are many lessons that I don't think he knew
he was teaching and I certainly didn't know I was learning. One profound learning was about immersion and devotion. My father was
a master woodworker. As I mentioned earlier, he built a thirty-foot
ketch in our backyard that I spent much of my youth on, sailing back
and forth across the Great South Bay off Long Island.

He would also spend hours in his basement workshop crafting

model sailboats. He would purchase blueprints for sailing ships from the 1800s and then, with infinite care and patience, build them to scale. One night, after dinner, he had vanished into his small kingdom of tools and I wandered quietly to sit on the top step of the basement stairs. I was eight or nine and he didn't know I was there. I watched him work carefully with tweezers, pulling the rigging in place on one of his model ships. I had never seen anyone so completely devoted to a detail. Something magical was unfolding. It was only years later that I realized what was happening there. My father was so immersed in building his model boat that he had slipped into the moment of everyone who had ever built a boat. He demonstrated that the first reward for immersion is the experience of Oneness. Excellence is just a byproduct of that immersion.

The second reward for immersion is that, in accessing the moment of everyone who ever built a boat, my father was being lifted by those eternal efforts. This is at the heart of resilience, that by being so thoroughly committed to what is ours to face and do, we slip into the stream of all those before us and after us and are lifted in that tide of life-force.

I've learned since that if I aim for excellence, I might do good work, but may never experience Oneness. But in the way that fire gives off heat, if I devote myself to being thoroughly immersed, I will, by the very nature of my effort, leave a trail of good work.

The third gift of immersion and devotion is that by being so thoroughly where we are, we paradoxically bring all of life to us. And so, once immersed, there is nowhere to go. The Impressionist legend Claude Monet is a steadfast example of immersion and devotion. He was strongly committed to painting exactly what he saw as a way to reveal the mysteries of light. It was the prime minister of France Georges Clemenceau who said that Monet and Van Gogh were like human microscopes, revealing the patterns of light and energy that exist below our surface understanding of things.

Across his long life of seeing, Monet developed cataracts in both eyes, eventually having surgery in 1923 at the age of eighty-three. The early surgeries were unsuccessful. But Monet never stopped painting, before and after the failed surgeries. Poignantly, he painted his masterful *Water Lilies* through the veil of his cataracts. He worked a lifetime honing his ability to see, only to paint his masterpiece through the breakdown of that sight. No matter what happened, he remained devoted to looking, seeing, and rendering what he saw, as accurately as he could. As such, Monet is our first example of the paradox of limitation.

On October 4, 1987, while I was in the midst of my journey with cancer, there was an early blizzard of thick, wet snow, which toppled hundreds of trees. The streets looked like a battlefield. At the time, I was facing very difficult decisions about what steps were next, none of which seemed good. Walking through the devastation of all those trees offered me a profound lesson that has stayed with me my whole life. Before the storm that day, the trees were in full color, thick with throngs of red and orange leaves. But no matter how brilliant, the trees came down because they held on to their leaves and could not escape the weight of the snow. I immediately became a student in the art of letting go, realizing the only way through my cancer journey was not to be brilliant but to be bare.

Another great Impressionist painter, Camille Pissarro, is instructive in how he faced adversity. In 1870, at the outbreak of the Franco-Prussian war, Pissarro urgently fled with his family to London, leaving all his paintings in his farmhouse outside of Paris. He returned after the war to find that of the fifteen hundred paintings he had created over twenty years, only about forty remained. The Prussians had used his canvases as doormats and as aprons when slaughtering sheep for their troops.

Devastated, Pissarro wandered about his dug-up farm, but finally resolved to begin again. And so, at the age of forty-one, Pissarro began to paint his masterful renderings of light that he saw cross the French countryside. All of his legendary work, which hangs in museums all over the world, was created from that moment forward. Pissarro confirms the need to always begin again, to believe in beginning, and to let what is taken be the threshold to all that can never be taken.

As my cancer journey progressed, I was overcome with fear, which I couldn't seem to silence or move through. One night, the great Chinese poet of the Tang dynasty, Tu Fu, visited me in a dream. He was sitting cross-legged on a beach near the water, making marks with a branch in the sand. I quickly approached and urgently asked, "How do I block the fear?" He ignored me, which made me more afraid. I moved closer and asked more firmly, "How do I block the fear?!" Without looking at me, he waved the branch above his head and said, "How does a tree block the wind?" With that, he disappeared. And I woke up.

Of course, a tree doesn't block the wind. It lets it through. So, while the fallen trees were teaching me that the only way to survive the storms of the world is to shed all that is not essential, Tu Fu was teaching me that the only way to survive inner storms is to let everything through.

Born in 1608 in London, John Milton was of the first generation of poets born after Shakespeare. He was a statesman, a diplomat, and an essayist. But his poetry was given no attention. Still, he remained faithful to his inner poetic voice, no matter how it was received. Due to untreated glaucoma, Milton's eyesight deteriorated until in 1652 at the age of forty-four, he went completely blind. This left him unmoored. But six years later, in 1658, depressed and impoverished, the blind poet, whom no one regarded as a poet, began dictating his epic poem *Paradise Lost* to a series of aides, including his daughters. With no assurance that what he was doing was worthwhile, he stayed faithful to this inner voice that kept leading him.

It took six more years to complete his epic poem, which was published in 1667 by Samuel Simmons in an edition that contained ten books and over ten thousand lines of poetry. It sold for three shillings. And though he could hold it, he could never see or read a word of it. Milton showed us that when you can't see outwardly, you can see inwardly. He was evidence of how singular each soul's vision is, the worth of which no one can bestow or take away.

Almost twenty-five years after nearly dying from cancer, I found myself with an ailment triggered by the damage I had undergone from chemo. Due to neuropathy, my stomach didn't recover from a nasty flu and my stomach wouldn't empty. This condition is known as gastroparesis. It can be chronic. I was blessed to have it resolve in seven months. During this time, I couldn't eat very much and lost a great deal of weight. In its unpredictable patterns, I would suddenly have a sharp pain, sometimes from having four bites instead of three. Common to those who suffer this condition, I began to be afraid to eat.

In Michigan, we are graced by Baltimore orioles for a few days each summer. That summer, on a glorious day, they appeared at our feeders, and I swiftly but quietly made my way to the window to see them. At that moment, I had one of those sharp pains. And there you have it, the paradox of limitation. I couldn't ignore or deny my pain, but I didn't want to miss the beauty of the orioles. Not just because of their small magnificence, but because their beauty was part of the medicine I needed in order to heal.

So, awkwardly, I felt my pain *and* received the orioles. Life was teaching me that, while our limitations force us to stop in front of beauty, we have to let all things in, in order to heal. That day, a deep truism presented itself, that we are asked to let beauty in *while* we are suffering. We are constantly challenged not to chase beauty as a way to run from our suffering, but to right-size our suffering by letting beauty mix with it. And, as much as we resist, limitations force us to be where we are.

During the Civil War, Walt Whitman received word that his brother George had been wounded in battle, and he raced to his side. His brother had only suffered minor wounds, but en route to finding his brother, Whitman saw the enormous cost of war. That suffering made him stay on as a volunteer medic on both sides.

At the same time, a determined young woman, Clara Barton, was also caring for the wounded. By the end of the war, she had handwritten more than 22,000 letters to the loved ones of those who had been wounded or died. She later went on to establish the Red Cross.

Both Walt Whitman and Clara Barton affirm what is possible when we dare to give when we think there is no more left to give. It is then that our deepest gifts appear.

A generation later, in 1910, outside of Paris, Django Reinhardt was born in a roaming caravan. He was a child prodigy on the banjo. Wherever the caravan traveled, Django played and quickly became well-known. But at the age of eighteen, he was caught in a fire that badly damaged the caravan. He himself was terribly burned. During eighteen months in the hospital, it was recommended that his right leg be amputated. He refused and learned how to walk with a cane. But more crucial was how the fourth and fifth fingers of his left hand were permanently frozen, making it impossible for him to play his banjo.

One day, Django's brother left a guitar by his bedside, which he reluctantly picked up. In time, he taught himself to play the guitar. And because he couldn't move his left hand along the fretboard from the neck to the body of the guitar, he began to discover a new way of chording, moving his lame fingers across the fretboard. This new way of chording became the foundation of modern jazz. As Monet saw his masterful *Water Lilies* through his cataracts, the limitations of Reinhardt's left hand led him to see the gateway to jazz.

There is one more heroic musician to consider and that is Beethoven. To me, he was heroic because he was an ordinary man caring for an extraordinary gift. Imagine that you are destined to bring music into the world that has never been heard before, and, at the same time, you are going deaf. While his gift was exhilarating, Beethoven's growing limitation was devastating. In 1802, he went to a small town outside of Vienna called Heiligenstadt, ostensibly for rest and solitude. Secretly, he was contemplating suicide, for the growing prospect of composing unprecedented music while not being able to hear it played was growing unbearable.

Beethoven, in fact, began to write a suicide note, which instead became a testament to resilience and endurance. Expressing the truth of his despair mysteriously empowered him to declare that he would go back to Vienna and make the most music he could with what he had for as long as possible. That document has become known as the *Heiligenstadt Testament*. He folded it and placed it in the top drawer of his desk in Vienna and proceeded to compose what is largely considered a decade of masterpieces.

Among those unparalleled compositions is a quartet for strings known as *Opus 131*. What makes this piece unique is that it has seven movements, not the traditional four, and there are no rest pauses throughout the entire composition. Now, even back then, professional string musicians would use those rest pauses to retune their instruments. For you can't play four movements, let alone seven, without your strings going out of tune. What, then, was Beethoven entreating by this? I believe he was saying that, no matter how we train or practice, life doesn't stop unfolding. And so, in music as in life, we will tune as we go. It won't be perfect. It won't always be in pitch, but we are called to make music anyway, imperfect but thorough.

These stories and the challenges they raise bring us back to our own lives and how we walk in the world. Just how do we listen to our limitations—and through our pain, discover the gifts that are waiting? There is no clear answer, but these stories offer a host of vows, which I invite you to personalize and live with, by making a commitment:

- to seek immersion over excellence in order to experience Oneness and to access resilience,
- to keep looking and to keep seeing things as they are,
- to stop clinging and to let go in the face of adversity in order to be bare and essential,
- to let difficult things through—like pain, fear, anxiety, and doubt—in order to draw strength from what can last,
- to honor the need to begin again, to believe in beginning, no matter what befalls us,

- to honor the need to journey inward and trust the voice of life as it speaks to each of us,
- to keep trying to give when we think we have no more left to give, as a means to uncover our deepest gifts,
- to persevere, that is, not to insist on what is lost, but to explore what new ground our limitation is pointing us to,
- and to accept that, devoted and immersed as we may be, we must tune as we go. We must forego perfection and come alive by being wholehearted.

Each of us will dream and each of us will stumble through storms while reaching for that dream. What we do next matters greatly. Sometimes, the stumble comes from our own stubbornness or blindness. Sometimes, the stumble comes from the merciless avalanche of events beyond our control. Either way, we are challenged like Pissarro to always begin again, to believe in beginning, and to let what is taken be the threshold to all that can never be taken.

Often, this deep imbuing of hope when knocked down is impossible to undertake alone. And so, there is no shame in asking for help in getting up, no shame in trying to turn our pain inside out. The great moments of living reside, not in banishing what goes wrong, but in unlacing trouble and weaving tapestries with the laces.

*We are constantly challenged not to chase beauty*
*as a way to run from our suffering, but to right-size*
*our suffering by letting beauty mix with it.*

## Questions to Walk With

- In your journal, describe a limitation you are struggling with. In what ways is this limitation preventing you from living and in what new direction is this limitation leading you? What new skills are you being asked to learn in order to step in that new direction?

- In conversation with a friend or loved one, describe someone you admire who has turned a limitation into a strength. What do you admire about this person? By what ways of being or doing have they met their limitation? Describe where these qualities live in you.

# Dropping the Scale

LIKE EVERYONE, I was taught that justice is blind, then given a scale to weigh and measure everything. Then, I was told on the sly that everyone peeks and puts their finger on the scale. And years later, after tumbling through the labyrinth of almost dying and waking up, I chanced upon the words of a man who lived fifteen hundred years ago who said that the urge in us to save a child from falling in a well is what makes us human. This was the Chinese philosopher Mencius and he used this image to define the notion of *ren*. It makes me think of my first dog, Saba, who, as pup in the snow for the first time, fell into an iced pond. My heart pounded and without any conscious choice, I was in that pond lifting her back into life as she was sinking. It makes me think of my oldest friend, Robert. When I came to after having a cancerous rib removed, he was over me with a washcloth on my head. It makes me think of St. Joseph's Oratory in Montreal where two hundred years ago a janitor was revealed as a healer. There is now a wall of crutches from all those he lifted back into life. It makes me think of the ancient shamans who somehow believed that to lay hands on the ill with an open heart would draw the toxins from their bodies and their minds. It makes me think of Jesus telling the wealthy merchant to drop his scale and enter Heaven now. The truth is that, like so many of us, I have been burdened by the hell of weighing, when Heaven waits in the things that matter that can't be weighed. In truth, I owe everything to those who have saved my life and yours, dropping everything to pull us from the fire.

*Heaven waits in the things that*
*matter that can't be weighed.*

## Questions to Walk With

- In your journal, tell the story of a time when someone put something down in order to offer you some care and how that saved you from a situation or from yourself.
- In conversation with a friend or loved one, describe a recent moment that stopped you and stunned you with its immediate sense of meaning. Without comparing this moment to anything else, how can you convey its impact?

# Restoring Our Kinships

———

Relationship is the fundamental truth
of this world of appearance.

—Rabindranath Tagore

This section explores the resources that will help us:

- provide each other enough warmth to thaw the encasement of technology,
- and rehabilitate our own storm-like tendencies to prevent being so volatile and destructive going forward.

All enduring knowledge is found in the web of relationship that holds the Universe together. Regardless of subject matter, each field of knowing is built on a fundamental Unity of Life that the work of relationship reveals. The great teacher Howard Thurman said, "There is a wholeness at the heart of humanity . . . that has its sway when all else fails." As a wave is only a wave when lifted by the sea, each soul is a presence in the world only when lifted by the wholeness at the heart of humanity. Our lifelong unfolding is an inner journey that lets us inhabit our kinship with that web of relationship that holds the Universe together. Though our particular paths will vary, all inner unfolding leads us to the same depth. The chapters in this section explore the difference between progress and incarnation, the well of being that waits below all names, the gift and press of miracle and tragedy, the never-ending practice of straying and returning, our kinship during adversity, and our irrepressible need to learn.

# Doing for Others,
# Seeing for Ourselves

A TRIBE MIGRATES west because they are being persecuted. They em-
igrate into the mountains. They settle on a plateau and, together, they
clear that part of the forest and build their homes, creating a settle-
ment, which the elder of the tribe names Crestview. In time, their
children are born where they have arrived, into a place where they
wake each day in a clearing with a view of the vastness.

The paradox at the center of this small story is that sometimes we
have to make pilgrimage to live in the open in order to have a view
of the vastness of life, and sometimes we are in debt to those before
us for what we assume is a birthright. Sometimes, we have to stand
on the commitment and hard work of others. Yet, there are other
passages in life that each of us has to journey through alone.

We can call the first process, progress, and the second, incarnation. In our long walk through time, we experience both. Progress
offers the rewards of one generation's efforts to the next. My father
didn't have to climb a mountain in the Rockies to see the sun set over
the Continental Divide because he could look at a photograph. And
I can get even closer by watching a video of it on the internet.

But something is lost for not making the climb ourselves. And
so, incarnation offers us the unrepeatable inner experience of direct
living that helps us inhabit what it means to be alive. While we can

benefit from those who have lived before us, no one can enter or make sense of this life but you.

Some people forego progress and become naturalists, believing that progress adds a layer to our living, which separates us from our basic nature. They return to the simplest form of outer living in order to refresh their inner experience of being alive. Others, like me, find a form of creative life to devote ourselves to in order to experience the same refreshed sense of being alive. As Claude Lévi-Strauss said, "The arts are the wilderness areas of the imagination surviving, like national parks, in the midst of civilized minds."

There is nothing inherently flawed about progress or incarnation. The ethic at the heart of progress is service—doing for others. And the ethic at the heart of incarnation is authenticity—seeing for ourselves. At our best, we can live an authentic life of service—doing for others, while seeing for ourselves. During times of pain, fear, or confusion, we often try to impose what we see on others and do only for ourselves. When beaten up by the uncertainty of life, we can give our birthright of seeing for ourselves away to a dominant parent or partner or to an orthodox tradition. But the most profound leaders are those who gather and share the gifts of progress with everyone. And the most profound teachers are those who offer the wisdom of the ages in support of everyone seeing for themselves.

The spiritual inventory, then, on any given day is: Are you doing more for others or yourself? Are you seeing through others or for yourself? Are you grateful for the progress you were born into? Are you directly living the one life you have been given? Are you teaching those around you how to see or to see what you see? Are you teaching those around you the difference between doing for others and doing for yourself? And are you learning the balance between the two?

It has also been my experience that doing for others has deepened my ability to see for myself and that seeing for myself has deepened my ability to do for others. This tells me that authenticity and service are inextricably linked, that being authentic empowers us to do good in the world and that doing good in the world, in turn, restores our authenticity. This reveals the ongoing bond between who we are and what we do, which is commonly known as integrity. I only know that I have grown from helping and being helped. I try to speak to this bond between giver and receiver in my poem called "Tell Me You Have Come:"

> The mystery is that
> whoever shows up
> when we dare to give
> has exactly what we need
> hidden in their trouble.

Like everyone before us, we each must find our own path into the clearing, where we can build a home near the vastness of life. And we each must pass on what we can, so that those who follow will have the chance to awaken their own lives, which no one but they can live. Like everyone who will follow us, we are each called to reveal and enliven the twin ethics of doing for others and seeing for ourselves.

*At our best, we can live an authentic life of*
*service—doing for others, while seeing for ourselves.*

## Questions to Walk With

- Describe a time when doing something for others deepened your ability to see for yourself, and a time when seeing for yourself deepened your ability to do for others.
- In conversation with a loved one or friend, describe an instance of progress from your grandmother's lifetime to your father's lifetime to your own in which you've benefited from the generation before you. Then, describe an instance of incarnation, some passage that your grandmother and father had to face, just as you do in your life.

# Miracle and Tragedy

To me, every hour of the light and dark is a miracle.

—Walt Whitman

Every life is a miracle and a tragedy, and these undeniable forces will, at times, overwhelm us. So, our first epic struggle is not to drown in the depths of tragedy and not to leave life through the transcendent pull of miracle. Our second noble struggle, which never ends, is to let the lightness of miracle and the groundedness of tragedy braid in our heart, so we can be thoroughly alive and live here now.

I am blessed to have lived through my own iterations of miracle and tragedy. And I can only attest to the mystery that miracle is not a dispensation from the press of our lives, but an uprising of inexplicable fortitude that informs us with the wherewithal to endure the riptide of life's forces when they catch us in their crosscurrents.

Humbly, while I have felt this fortitude from time to time, it is not mine. Any more than the lift of an eagle's wing is his alone or the truth that comes from our heart is ours alone. We are at best surprised carriers of a grace that jump-starts our instinct to give wherever care is needed.

Still, we cannot escape the interplay of both miracle and tragedy, any more than shells can escape the lift and dash of the surf. And so, we must find a way to feel the break in what breaks and the wonder in the opening it makes in us and those around us. None of this is easy or fully comprehensible, only knowable at the root level of experience.

Imagine it this way. Sometimes, the life-giving downpour will snap a limb on its way to releasing spring. And once the storm has vanished, the flowers under the trees come alive and open. And sometimes, a boy drawn by their wild color will find the broken limb among the flowers and bring it home to secretly carve a walking stick for his bent and smiling grandfather who is as crooked as the fallen limb.

From outside the story, this seems a sweet happenstance. But when it's our turn to be the snapped limb, then God seems merciless and life has no meaning. This is true, in part, because when we close our eyes, the world of light seems lost and gone—as long as we refuse or forget how to open our eyes and see again. As real and painful as tragedy is, it is always as close to miracle as the opening of an eye or a heart or a mind. It's as challenging as it is true that the only way through tragedy is to open up and let the lost world of light in again.

Often, this second opening is too difficult to do alone and we need the help of others. But whether we open and see again or not, miracle and tragedy are forever linked, the way day and night will always follow each other.

Nonetheless, within life's passages, it is difficult to stay open to miracle when in the throes of tragedy and difficult to stay open to tragedy when in the ease of miracle. But staying open to both expands our consciousness and deepens our heart. For it is the majestic whole of life's unfolding power that lifts us and dashes us again and again until we are rearranged into an unforeseen aspect of beauty.

*We cannot escape the interplay of*
*both miracle and tragedy.*

## Questions to Walk With

- In your journal, explore your own struggle between extreme transcendence, being pulled too much out of life, and extreme groundedness, being ground too much into the circumstances of life.
- In conversation with a friend or loved one, describe a recent time when both miracle and tragedy washed through your life.

# Our Need to Learn

Those who wake are the students.
Those who stay awake are the teachers.
How we take turns.

—MN

EVERY CULTURE ON Earth has a name for teacher: the Hindu *guru,* the Yiddish *rebbe,* the Chinese *sensei,* the Arabic *mundaris,* the Vietnamese *giao vien,* the Turkish *ogretmen,* the Welsh *athro,* the Lithuanian *mokytojas,* the Italian *insegnante,* the Czech *ucitel,* the Norwegian *laerer,* the Yoruba *oluko,* and the Zulu *uthisha.*

In English, the word *teacher* goes back to Old English, meaning "to show or point out." The word *teacher* is related to the word *token,* which means "a visible or tangible representation of a fact, quality, or feeling." And so, the long history of teaching is deeply embedded in the vow to be a window to all that matters. Toward that end, teaching has always relied on the art of demonstration. The greatest teachers offer examples not instructions. The greatest teachers lead students to their teacher within.

Regardless of subject matter, teaching is a noble ferrying between the shores of knowing and not knowing. In this way, each particular field of knowledge is a facet of the unknowable prism that is the Mystery of Life. And each field of knowledge serves as a way to manifest truth in the world.

Across history, education has always been concerned with discovering meaning and building tools from that meaning and learning how to use them. Yet, despite all our efforts to empower free thinking, we often impart—sometimes consciously, sometimes unconsciously—what tools are to be used for. This is often an imposition of values. In showing how to use a hammer, we inevitably convey what should be built with a hammer. In showing how to think, we inevitably convey which ideas are worth thinking. In showing how to pray, we inevitably convey who should be prayed to and what should be prayed for. The most liberating teachers encourage students to follow their hearts and live by their own values. This speaks to the right and need to determine our own usefulness.

It's interesting that the word *embarrass* means "feeling awkward or ashamed." The word comes from the Spanish *embarazar,* which comes from the Portuguese *baraço,* which means a "halter," the bit placed in the mouth of a horse. At its deepest, embarrassment is a sign that we are not being authentic or true to who we really are. And not being authentic makes us susceptible to being led around by others. Embarrassment, then, is a helpful signal that someone is putting a halter in our mouth, trying to lead us somewhere.

Once we recognize that we are being led astray, we can realign our being and purpose. How? By cleaning the inner windows of the eye, mind, and heart, we can restore our authenticity. And only when authentic can we feel our being and see our purpose. Over a lifetime, loving these windows is the work of inner education that returns us to the place of true meeting where we can experience the Oneness of Reality. It is the tending of these windows—building and repairing them—that keeps us present and real.

On a personal level, it is the life of question and expression that cleans these windows. For each true question opens a threshold between a person's interior and the Mystery of Life. In the world of meaning and being, questions are not asked to be answered, but to reveal a trailhead that exists between our depths and the world. We don't answer trails, we walk them. So, asking true questions is a tender and lasting way to invite others to walk with us on the trail of our lives.

As we meet reality, every feeling becomes a teacher. Consider that, given time, every flame releases its light, and every surface touched by water will soften. Likewise, given time, every feeling that rises within us will release its light, and every hardness if held will soften. This is the chief work of expression: to give our feelings time so they can teach us how to lighten and soften.

Here are two stories that speak to this deeper, lasting form of education. The first comes from India. For centuries in India, baby elephants were tethered with a small rope tied to a slender tree. Later, when fully grown and massive, it was discovered that, if chained to a tree, they could snap the chain or rip the tree out as they wished. But if a fully grown elephant was tethered again with a small rope to a small tree, it would honor that tether. There are many ways to look at this. From the surface, it seems a trick of training by which to contain an elephant's movement. From the inside, though, the tether can be seen more as a slender root than a leash. When chained, the elephant feels a constraint on its freedom and breaks that chain easily. But being lightly tethered, as when it was small, seems more a reminder of its beginnings. In this sense, the tether is there so the elephant won't get lost. Of course, it matters greatly to what center we are tethered.

Symbolically, this suggests that there might be slender, but essential roots that tie us to the foundational Wholeness of Life. And, if given those ties early on, they will forever remind us of the elusive Source we were so close to in the beginning. This brings to mind *spiritual tethers* that might keep us from getting lost when we are fully grown and massive. What might they be? And to what center are we tied? This is the province of spiritual education. And while teachers can point out our foundations, our spiritual tethers are very personal. Only the truth-seeker can know what these are and make a practice of honoring them.

The second story comes from Bethesda, Maryland. There is a center in Bethesda that promotes people in their search for Wholeness. It is called Shalem. It was the working home of the late psychiatrist and author Gerald May. During a visit there years ago, Jerry told me that the center was named after the phrase in Deuteronomy that says, "You must love God with your whole heart." In that phrase, the word for *whole* is *shalem,* a cognate of *shalom.* The word carries a sacred question that is before us all: What kind of Wholeness enables us to experience God? This is a question that we can't problem-solve but only live into. The deeper we live this question, the more we discover, as Gerald May says, that consciousness is a renewable natural resource which, despite all our attempts to clarify, rushes everything living together.

In deep ways, loving God with our whole heart is the same as experiencing Wholeness through being fully human. When Goethe has Faust make his deal with the devil, we have come to read that arrangement through the lens of ambition and greed of all types, including a greed for knowledge. As such, we see Faust trade his flaws and mistakes for virtues not rightly his. But a closer look at the original German reveals a different arrangement.

The physicist Arthur Zajonc tells us that Faust's deal with the devil is not "If I make a *mistake,* you can have my soul. . . ." More accurately, Faust says, "If I stop *aspiring,* you can have my soul. . . ." This reveals a pivotal difference. We are human and will always make mistakes. But if we stop aspiring, we forfeit our souls.

*Aspire,* from the Latin, means "to breathe." When we aspire to specific things—I want a million dollars, I want a yacht—we fall prey to worldly ambition. But when we aspire to live, holding nothing back, we breathe more fully and come alive. And while it makes good sense to look twice while crossing a road, in the world of meaning and being, hesitation closes the mouths of angels.

Reflecting on all this, I happened to watch a heron on a lake. The heron was waiting, balanced on its long left leg, waiting to see through the water. I think it was waiting to dive for food. While waiting, it could see through. But each time it pecked, the water splattered and the clarity was broken. It had to wait to see where to dive next. It did this for Eternity like a person trying through their humanness to live off the deep.

*The long history of teaching is deeply embedded*
*in the vow to be a window to all that matters.*

## Questions to Walk With

- In your journal, describe one thing you need to currently learn that will help you come alive and live more fully. What steps can you take to start learning this?
- In conversation with a friend or loved one, tell the story of someone who unexpectedly became a teacher for you. You may have encountered them in life as well as in school. What is the enduring thing that they have taught you?

# Below All Names

To see is to forget the name of the thing one sees.

—Paul Valéry

I was interviewed by Ashton Gustafson in the fall of 2019. We were talking over Skype about the unexpected gift that comes when we can touch life under the veil of names we give it. I was in my study, looking out my window at the large maples and oaks that sway their branches before me every day. I said, "When I lean in and am fully present, holding nothing back, any moment can be restorative—opening its point of connection to all life."

I went on, "Even now, if I can be present with nothing in the way, this old tree out my window conveys the life-force it contains below the name of *tree*. When this open and present, no matter how briefly, the *tree* sheds its name and stands before me in its original thing-ness—as an undeniable growth of wood bursting from the ground, twisting skyward, only to sprout these thin, flat, wafer-like blades, which the air in its constant movement lifts and drops. The miracle of its being is palpable and through the essence of any one thing, we can feel the presence of all things."

It was then that Ashton said, "This reminds me of what the French poet Paul Valéry points to when he says, 'To see is to forget the name of the thing one sees.'" For all I've read, I had never come across this line. It stirred me. For to truly see is to look with our wholehearted presence until things appear in their original state before human beings began to pin names on everything. Such seeing returns us to the pulse of life that lives below all names.

Thirty-three years ago, I remember waking after having a rib removed from my back, and in that stir of broken wakefulness, I forgot my name. Or rather, I dropped beneath the silhouettes others had drawn around me into the vibrant sense of life that exists below all labels and definitions. Ever since, a deep part of me has lived below all names. And this has been the well I return to in order to drink directly from life. This is where I retrieve the poems. Ironically, the only things worth writing about are those that can't be named or put into words. But we can point to them.

This is the true purpose of naming. For a name serves as a threshold we can *enter* to *experience* the unnamed essence of a thing. However, all too often, we rely on a name to *represent* the thing, and we accept the representation of the thing for the thing itself. But the reward for trying to give expression to things and experiences is that the naming opens us to a *relationship* with the thing named.

We all know the shapes of the states that constitute America. We can draw any state on a napkin and easily recognize it. But when flying in a plane, those state lines are not there. We only see the unbroken continent in its oneness. Likewise, you may can fruit and shelve it in your basement. But the label is not the fruit. In truth, we often thwart ourselves when we mistake the map for the continent or the label of the container for the fruit the jar contains. We do this with love, heartbreak, and grief as well. In our fear, we use names to contain these emotions and put them on a shelf. Then, we store them in our basement and think that by handling the containers, we've digested what's in them.

Yet when we can live below all names, however briefly, we are returned to an Original Presence that sustains all life. This is how, as Blake says, we can "see a world in a grain of sand." Or how the reach of one exhausted hand lifting someone who has fallen can hold the essence of care. For when thoroughly present, one gesture of kindness can reveal and carry all gestures of kindness.

In our humanness, the vast turbulence of life throws us under and rocks us about. Our ever-present challenge is to see through the turbulence with our steadfast presence until the name *surprise* dissolves into the vibration of what is close but not yet revealed. It is through a perseverance of being that we are dropped beneath the veil of names. Once there, we inhabit a more felt and lasting way, which reveals this fundamental law of Spirit: that everything emanates its own aspect of beauty, which when touched can animate us with the irrepressible energy of life.

For under all our plans and goals and secret desires, the heart only wants to inhabit its aliveness. This is the seed of our deeper self. And whether we get what we want or not, the life-force within us only wants to stream from Source to mouth, the way a river doesn't really care where it goes or how long it takes for its water to get where it's going. Likewise, the deeper self only wants light in its belly and it will wait for us to exhaust ourselves of all our blueprints and designs. It will wait for us to simply feed it the energy we call love.

One of the things that poetry—the unexpected utterance of the soul—has taught me is that the aliveness that lives below all names waits for us to say yes to life. And saying yes to life lets us love ourselves. These three presences are forever connected: what lives below all names, saying yes to life, and loving ourselves. They lead us to our worth.

> *The only things worth writing about*
> *are those that can't be named.*

## Questions to Walk With

- In your journal, describe the difference in your openness of mind and heart when you are busy and when you have nowhere to go. Detail the conditions that enable you to stay open. How can you inhabit these conditions of openness when you are busy?

- Go for a walk with a friend or loved one and note at least five details that seem to hold the same essential feel of life-force that lives under all names. Discuss these moments of life-force, looking for the common wisdom they share.

# Straying and Returning

No one is so advanced in prayer
that they do not have to return to the beginning.

—St. Teresa of Ávila

We are all challenged to both survive and thrive. But if we only survive without a way to thrive, what's the point? Yet, survival is essential. So, we must make sure that we can thrive without putting ourselves completely at risk. In daily terms, only you can know what a healthy balance looks like.

Over the years, I have experienced a corridor of clarity in the center of surviving and thriving, which I inevitably stray from in fear and must return to through risk. But in our anticipation and worry, we add layers to our fear. These added layers keep us from being fully alive. And so, we have to part the layers of fear and worry in order to return to living our life.

From time to time, I have found it helpful to take an inventory around the nature of my fear and worry. I try to discern the gap between the level of fear and worry I am carrying and the actual risks being asked of me. This helps me see the true choices that are before me.

All the while, everything in this mysterious journey points to our appreciation that life is precious. In fact, the word *appreciate* means "to move toward what is precious."

This has been a guiding principle for me: to discern the way, as accurately as I can, and to keep moving toward what is precious. In so doing, we must never doubt the wisdom of our heart.

Let's look more closely at the nature of straying and returning. At an elemental level, we stray from the light and return to the light. Just as the Earth spins on its axis, our effort in life turns us around a timeless Center that goes nowhere but which holds everything together. And wonder and awe are the tug and ache of how we turn around the Center of Life. Wonder and awe are the tug and ache of being alive. This pull around the Center of Life is a fundamental form of straying and returning for all human beings.

## The Spiritual in the Human

Earlier, I mentioned that Pierre Teilhard de Chardin said, "We are not human beings having a spiritual experience. We are spiritual beings having a human experience." There are many ways to unpack this. If we go through life assuming that we contain things, we tend to see ourselves as a container. This leads to seeing everything in our own image, as we often try to make everything fit the container that is us. And so, we tend to make mirrors of everything we encounter; seeing wind, rain, cars, trouble, the moon, even Spirit as reflections of ourselves.

But when we can acknowledge that we are spiritual beings having a human experience, that something larger and deeper is moving through us, then the mysteries begin to open, as soon as we admit that we are contained in something infinite and inexpressible.

Assuming we are a container limits life to the sense that one iris, though obedient to the laws of nature, is a beautiful anomaly, a single blossom unto itself, rising out of nothing, no more, no less. But acknowledging that we are part of an endless Universe that, as Einstein suggests, recycles matter into energy over and over, this opens us to the miracle that the energy-of-seed-becoming-stem-becoming-blossom, the very Spirit of flowers, enters this iris—just as the iris before it and in concert with the lineage that informs every iris.

This is a beautiful way to understand love. Though we choose whether or not to act on love, we do not create love, any more than a hawk creates the air that lifts it. Rather, the indestructible energy of soul breaking through our loneliness blossoms before another whose whole purpose of being is suddenly to join us—just as every living soul before us and in concert with all who ever loved. It is our courage of openness—to put down a limiting view and to let in a larger one—that makes all this possible.

Imagine. If we are aspects of Spirit having a human experience, like the Spirit of plants becoming particular flowers, then no one owns a particular embodiment of Spirit. Rather, who we are is enlivened in our lifetime by part of a larger Spirit greater than any one person. So, if Spirit spreads like pollen, then to be reincarnated is to be the unknowing carrier of spiritual seed.

In this, we are not being reborn as someone who lived before us, but more as someone who in our aliveness is keeping the common energy of essence in circulation. And so, we unknowingly do our part in advancing a spiritual lineage. Not by consciously passing down traditions, though that has its place in the preservation of wisdom. But by daring to blossom completely into who we truly are, we resurrect and reincarnate the light of the world in our brief time on Earth.

A deep, recurring form of straying and returning is this endless journey between the rush of aliveness we feel when authentically here and the need to re-find that aliveness when we stray from our direct experience of life. When we are numb, we need to find a way to inhabit our heart and mind. When we have lost our way, we need to find an embodiment that can reconnect us to the miracle of life. Finding the courage and working the courage to inhabit our connection to the living reservoir of all Spirit empowers us on our way, the way a fish is swept along when finding the swift current in the middle of a stream.

## Lost in the Straying

Sometimes when we stray, we can get lost in the straying. When we get stuck in the straying, we grow confused and out of balance, and lose our way to return. The Hopi tribe has a name for being stuck in the imbalance, *koyaanisquatsi,* which is Hopi for "crazy life, life out of balance," a state of chaos and agitation that begs for another way of living.

Aspects of life that keep us out of balance include: not listening, judging and comparing, chasing happiness, and avoiding life.

Listening always feeds the fire of aliveness which is illuminating, while not listening always feeds the fire of circumstance which burns us up. Listening is always life-giving, while not listening is always life-draining. When we stop listening, we start living in ways that clog our mind and heart.

When not listening, we land in the confining realms of judgment and comparison, which only muffle our sense of aliveness. As Aldous Huxley remarked:

> Judgment and comparison commit us irrevocably to duality. Only choiceless awareness can lead to non-duality, to the reconciliation of opposites in a total understanding and a total love.

Once in the snare of judgment and comparison, we start to believe that life is other than where we are. Then, we start chasing after life, as if we are not alive. The British poet William Cowper (1731–1800) phrased the condition of chasing this way:

> I see that all are wanderers, gone astray
> Each in [our] own delusions; [we] are lost
> In chase of fancied happiness, still wooed
> And never won.

All these aspects of imbalance impinge on our presence. And without authentic presence, we tend to avoid life. The different ways that we avoid life include: withdrawing, hiding, running away, shutting down, having an agenda, changing the subject, projecting, being quick to be offended, and getting angry. Each is a different way of not seeing and not listening.

A painful example of avoidance is the medieval doctor Sydenham who fled the plague, denying that he was a doctor and refusing to help. Inevitably, we are challenged not to leave but to stay present and see our way through.

Clearly, the antidotes to these aspects of imbalance are to refine our practices of listening, suspending judgment and comparison, to accept that happiness is always waiting where we are, and facing life.

When we can stay present, we can resist these aspects of imbalance. When present, there is no peace like the moment of stillness that rises from the foundation of our own experience of Life and Spirit. We may forget that we are alive at times and be quite blind at other times, but once returning to the felt sense of what matters, it is with us forever.

## Inflammation of the Eyes

Massage historian Robert Noah Calvert tells the story of a Dine man of distinction who was losing his vision from the inflammation of his eyes, believed to have come about from looking upon sacred masks with an irreligious heart. The compelling instruction in this story is that looking upon sacred things with an irreligious heart can lead to blindness. Because when we look upon sacred things with irreverence, a veil begins to form between us and the life-force that inhabits the world.

The Buddhists call this drift from seeing things as they are the veil of illusion. The Taoists speak of the opaqueness that forms between us and things as they are as the seed of evil. The protestant theologian Paul Tillich speaks of sin as our separation from reality. All these notions confirm that irreverence or a lack of holding things sacredly can lead to a loss of true sight. I have often made reference to the Chinese wisdom from *The Doctrine of the Mean* that says, "Given sincerity, there will be enlightenment." This is to say that given reverence, there will be a deep seeing that sustains. There is a relationship between reverence and truth. While irreverence and separation cause blindness, only reverence and compassion can restore true seeing.

So, the Dine man who was losing his sight went to the shaman of his tribe and asked to be healed. For only sacred touch could cure him. And the first step in healing, always, is to humbly ask to be healed. It took eight days. After a day of solitude and silence, the shaman rubbed the invalid with the horn of a mountain sheep and then with a piece of hide from between the horns. On the fourth day, the invalid drank pine-needle water and then bathed in it, while the shaman massaged his right leg with the sheep's horn and hide. On the eighth day, the shaman placed his hands on the soles of his patient's feet while hooting. Then the heart of the invalid was touched with the palm of the shaman's right hand, his left hand pressing on his patient's back. The body was pressed this way four times, each with a loud cry. Finally, after touching the figures in a sand-painting, the shaman touched the forehead of the invalid, and pressed his head four times. By the next day, the patient had regained his sight.

What can we glean from the shaman's healing of the sightless man? What does this ancient ritual tell us about our return to inner health?

First, we must ask to be healed. In so doing, we must admit that we are not well. As long as we deny our difficulty, there is no chance of a return to health. Next, we have to still ourselves so we can sink below the noise of all straying.

Then, we are ready to be touched by the things that roam the Earth and the things that grow from the Earth. The horn and hide of the mountain sheep represent the need to be renewed by the hard and soft instruments of primal living.

Finally, the shaman touches the soles of the patient's feet to strengthen his walk in the world. Then, presses the patient's heart and back four times, possibly once for each of the four directions, to solidify the connection between the patient's heart and backbone, so he can return to being a strong conduit of life-force in his days.

At last, the shaman honors the impermanence of all life by touching the figures in a sand-painting before touching the invalid's forehead and pressing his head four times, as a way to compress the entire healing process of straying and returning into the invalid's consciousness. After returning to what a fragile miracle living is, the man wakes the next day with his sight restored.

It would do us well to take these healing stages and personalize each in order to facilitate the restoration of our own sight. And, as the Dine man can't heal himself alone, we need each other to reclaim our deeper sight.

## Practices of Return

To repair means "to pair again," "to rejoin," "to put back together." The effort to pair again and rejoin is crucial to any practice of returning. Perennially, three practices return us to the radiance in all things: authenticity, slowness, and, as mentioned earlier, the suspending of judgment.

When authentic, when walking in our presence without pretense, we thin and remove whatever film there is between us and our direct experience. Then, there is little or nothing between our inner life and outer circumstance. When slowing down enough, we can actually slip into the spaces between things where life-force resides. And suspending judgment allows for life to reach us beneath our assumptions and conclusions where we are still touchable and teachable.

There is a Hindu greeting, *drishde,* practiced by the Brahma Kumaris, through which love and spiritual power is given, from one to another, through the eyes. This transmission between souls is generated from a place of presence and authenticity. It is believed this act of generosity can return us to the Living Center of Life and repair the fissures in our humanity.

So, there are many ways to return when we stray, and each must be personalized. To summarize a few:

- We need to listen so we can stay open to all aspects of life.
- We need to suspend judgment and comparison so we can be touched by life.
- We need to stop chasing happiness and accept that life is where we are.
- We need to commit to facing life.
- We need to admit when we are not well and ask to be healed.
- We need to restore our connection to the things that roam the Earth and the things that grow from the Earth.
- We need to rejoin the life of our heart with the life of our backbone, so we can act with heart in the world.
- We need to restore our deeper sight by reclaiming our authenticity.
- We need to accept our place in the impermanent cycle of life.
- We need to slow down so that the very pulse of life can animate us and pass through us.
- And we need to practice the transmission of love and spiritual power, eye to eye, and heart to heart.

## Finding Our Way Home

I have a friend who just finished eighteen months of traveling around the world. He embarked on this journey at the close of many years of living in the United States. As he traveled, he didn't have a home. He knew he would settle somewhere else for the next phase of life, but wasn't sure where. His trip was intended to offer him some inner reflection about where that might be. He has since settled in Vienna, where he has been living for about four months.

What he profoundly reports is that traveling without a place to return to, without a central place or home to travel from, proved to be very difficult and disorienting. He found himself expending enormous energy to stay centered, trying to imagine a core locale from which his changing experiences could be understood. He was not just speaking of a physical home, but of a relational home, an inner home. He was referring to the need for an inner reference point, a core location of Source. Without this center, tangible or not, it is difficult to make sense of our experience. Without an inner reference point, we are lost forever in straying, never able to return to the well of the living.

The truth is, of all the places I'll never get to, being here—in the presence opened in this moment—is the hardest, sweetest journey I've ever made. It is here to which we are called to return. Throughout time, the mystics of all traditions bear witness to the inevitability of our straying from what matters and the holiness of our return.

Consider the contemporary mystic eden ahbez (1908–1995). He was an American songwriter whose nomadic life led to his all-embracing perspective. His chosen last name, *ahbez,* comes from a biblical name whose root means "to gleam." His full chosen name reflects the notion of returning to a place of origin that allows us to shine or gleam.

In his song "The Wanderer," from his album *Eden's Island* (1960), ahbez affirms that "Heaven and Earth are open cathedrals [in which] all are crowned by love and bound by loss . . . [there] I am everyone and no one."

In the open cathedral of life on Earth, we are all, when blessed, everyone and no one. For straying and returning is inborn to the human journey. And the vow to be who we are is nothing less than the unending effort to return to a place of origin that allows us to shine or gleam.

*When authentic, when walking in our presence*
*without pretense, we thin and remove whatever film*
*there is between us and our direct experience.*

## Questions to Walk With

- In your journal, explore how you can personally refine your practices of listening, suspending judgment and comparison, accepting that happiness is where you are, and facing life. What steps can you take in each practice to help you get closer to life?

- In conversation with a friend or loved one, describe your own history of straying from what matters and returning to what brings you alive.

# Our Kinship During Adversity

THE QUTANG GORGE is the shortest and most spectacular of China's Three Gorges. Along its sheer and narrow slopes are ancient pathways. Since the earliest days, boats going downstream used oars to invoke some steerage. But going upstream, human-powered oars were no match for the rapid currents of the Yangtze River. Thus, workers, harnessed to a towrope on the stony slopes, hauled the boats upstream. In time, these haulers created a path along the steep cliffs to walk on. In this way, footpaths were carved and worn into the cliffs next to the river. Eventually, narrow towpaths were systematically built during the Western Han dynasty (206 BC–AD 220) and maintained and improved until the middle of the twentieth century. Even today haulers can be seen towing boats as in the photograph on the next page.

These worn steps along the deep and fast currents of the Yangtze River are symbolic of another ancient pathway: the one we always find against all odds when the heart is stirred to reach beyond itself and haul those caught in the stream. No one really knows why we do this or why it is not held up as more ingenious and courageous. For it is both. Hauling others upstream in times of need is life-sustaining for all involved. This inexplicable care, at the heart of all relationship, wears a narrow path near the fast-moving current of life. It is there that we take turns hauling and towing each other through sudden turns in the river.

The Ancient Pathway along the Qutang Gorge in China

Another example of our ancient response to adversity is the Yotsugi-dōri Canal in Japan, made famous by the great woodblock master Hiroshige in a compelling print from his legendary *One Hundred Famous Views of Edo.* The canal, north of Tokyo, was created in response to the Great Fire of 1657 in Meireki as a way to bring water to the devastated village. Caring citizens would walk on the bank towing small, slender boats with food and water to those in need. A hundred years later, in the 1770s, the towboats hauling water to the Great Fire evolved into a ferry service where people onshore would tow those in small boats up the canal for a price.

But the emergence of towboats in response to the Great Fire of 1657 illustrates, literally and symbolically, how in times of adversity and deep pilgrimage we need to take turns towing and being towed. Eventually, of necessity, we haul each other: one of us on shore towing the other; one of us stunned and battered, accepting the need to be cared for.

The first lesson of the Qutang Gorge and the Yotsugi-dōri Canal is that the things that replenish us are found in the center of the current. Though from time to time, if left alone, the sudden, rapid current will take us down. So the second lesson is that sometimes we can better do the hard work of making our way upstream, if a loved one or ally can tow us for a while. This speaks to the covenant of all community: that we are interdependent and in constant need of each other.

In understanding our kinship during adversity, there is one more example to consider. In his book of poems *Fully Empowered,* the great Chilean poet Pablo Neruda offers a small poem called "Summary" in which he is grateful for the paradox that joins peace and trouble. Neruda confirms:

> That is why—water on stone—my life was always
> singing its way between joy and obligation.

As anyone who's ever wandered by a stream knows, there is no song without water and stone playing off each other. It is the same with the hauling and towing of each other in times of need. We are fragile, tensile creatures who can drown in obligation while pining for joy, as well as run from all service while insisting on a very private happiness. Yet when moved to reach out and help, it is our care pulling another through trouble that releases the song we know as resilience.

At any moment in our tumble on Earth, we can find ourselves in need of help. At any moment, the wave of life's circumstance can

*Towboats along the Yotsugi-dōri Canal*, Hiroshige

swell with force until we or those near are swept under. This turbulent moment is what compels compassion into the open, the way every moment of darkness calls for light to fill it. When it is our turn, whether we are humbly towed or called to do the towing, the song of life waits in the inevitable flow of love over suffering, of acceptance over hardship, and of joy over obligation.

*When moved to reach out and help, it is*
*our care pulling another through trouble that*
*releases the song we know as resilience.*

## Questions to Walk With

- In your journal, describe a time when someone reached from shore to offer you a tow in times of need. What transpired between you and how are you different for being helped in this way?
- In conversation with a friend or loved one, describe your own balance between joy and obligation. How do the two reside in you and how do they inform each other in your heart?

# The Restorative Nature of Belief

IN MY THIRTIES, as I've mentioned, I almost died from a rare form of lymphoma but the tumor in my skull bone vanished—a miracle no one could explain. Everyone tried to claim its disappearance for their particular facet of the Mystery: it was Jesus, Moses, Allah, the power of my mind, the insistence of my heart, my will, my surrender, the care of my loved ones, the randomness of chance, it was the healing power of our ancestors. Yet when light floods a prism, the power of its illumination does not reside in any one facet, but in the source of light bringing the prism alive. Having been restored and brought alive, I cannot argue with the praise for any one facet of my healing but am humbled to say yes to all, as each is evidence of the Source under all causes.

Because of this, I've come to see that everything is saturated with the spirit of life and our belief in life is the conduit that releases life's power. Our belief animates us through whatever we choose to believe in. Our focused belief is the magnifying glass of heart that can ignite the inherent life-force residing in any particular aspect of life. And so, that we believe is always more important than what we believe in.

Whether you believe in meditation or service or exercise, whether you commit to climbing the largest mountains in the world or to cultivating the various forms of roses in your garden, whether you collect historic stamps from many countries or search out every re-cording of "April in Paris"—whatever the particulars that draw our belief into being—it is the authenticity of our care that is essential.

The problem arises when we impose what we believe in on others rather than support the personal engagement of belief and how it can transform and restore us. For what reveals our common bond is the acceptance and inquiry into each other's experience of belief.

In Buddhism, *saddha* is the word for faith, which translates as "resting the heart in what is true." This is the threshold to a life of authenticity. And as a single breath is at the center of any practice of breathing, our belief in what is true is the single, recurring act that animates our practice of native faith.

For belief, when experienced as a teacher without a name, enables us to enliven a kinship between the living part and the living Whole. Such sustained care begins to heal us. With humility, it is not our place to denounce what others believe in, but to use the sincerity of their example as an encouragement to find our own particular inlet into the Mystery of Life.

Ultimately, belief is a human inlet through which life-force visits us. It moves through us more than originates in us. The impact of belief resides more in how it informs our aliveness than in tracking its results. When a flower or plant dies, it does not mean that photosynthesis has ceased to exist. And when the lightbulb in the kitchen burns out, it does not mean that electricity is a false god. Likewise, when what I hope and pray for does not come to pass, it does not mean that the indestructible life of Spirit has collapsed. Under all our trials and blessings, it is our belief that engenders the undeniable regeneration of life connecting to other life. For belief is a state of aliveness to experience, not a place of certainty to land in; more a thorough commitment to life than our devotion to a religious principle.

I have come to understand belief as the animation of Spirit by the life-force that carries it. And the animation of Spirit in the world is much more important than the conclusions of any believer or the worship of any object of belief. As the life of a fish depends on the ocean, the life of any believer depends on the endless sea of Spirit he or she swims in. So, allow yourself to be touched by life. And once touched, allow your heart to respond with care. Then, regardless of what you call it, the synapse of touch and care will spark a longer conversation between your heart and the Universe.

> *Belief is a state of aliveness to experience,*
> *not a place of certainty to land in.*

## Questions to Walk With

- In your journal, tell the story of a moment when light revealed something you hadn't seen or felt until the light brought it to you, and describe how this has informed your belief in light.
- In conversation with a friend or loved one, describe some activity that has rewarded you for the attention you have given to it. It might be gardening, walking in nature, working with wood, playing an instrument, listening to music, or listening to the stories of others. What has this activity given you for your attention?

# The Rush of Life

In our era, the road to holiness necessarily passes through the world of action.

—Dag Hammarskjöld

THIS SECTION EXPLORES the resources that will help us:

- shore up and preserve our foundations from being eroded and washed away.

The flow of life is always moving through us and around us. Think of the thousands of surfs around the world all crashing and receding in infinite variety—all at once. Think of the wind rushing through thousands of trees, in valleys, on mountainsides, along highways and country roads—all at once. Think of the thousands of songs and cries leaving our mouths every day around the world—all at once. This is just part of the rush of life which renews us and overwhelms us by turns. A very human challenge is how to relate to the rush of life, how to put ourselves in a position to be renewed by it and how to endure its moments of overwhelm. The chapters in this section try to understand how we are most alive in the thick of the struggle, how the mind works as an inlet and not a container, how we are always torn between looking and not looking, how we are ever called into uncharted waters, and how we constantly work toward accepting that life is always where we are.

# In the Thick of It

THE TIMES SEEM dire, at times apocalyptic. Wildfires are rampant. Hurricanes are the size of states. And racism continues to rear its ugly head. Will we survive? Will humanity survive? I believe we will. Not because I deny the truth of these difficulties. Not because we try to reframe everything into a better light. But because all things are true. All things are not fair or just, but all things are true.

And it is the call of each generation to make sure that we choose love over fear and kindness over cruelty, one more time. We are all capable of both. This is why it is imperative to accept that each generation and each life takes its turn in opening one more time than closing, in giving one more time than taking, in standing in integrity in the thick of it all.

While it is true that the planet could burn up, and that we might make ourselves extinct, I am anchored in the knowledge that we have been on this dark precipice before. And witnessing the history of the soul, I believe in incarnation more than progress. As I explored earlier, progress calls for us to leave the world in a better place than we found it, while incarnation is the inevitable process of facing life and living life that no one can escape. And though progress lets us take a lift to the top of a mountain instead of climbing it, it is the work of incarnation that calls for each person to open their eyes and see. While our efforts at bettering life may be fleeting, our efforts in facing life are more lasting.

And so, it is our turn to put out the fires and to quiet the storms and to open our hearts beyond our prejudice. The pain of needless suffering will always be with us. Yet we can mitigate its sharpness by enlarging our sense of things and by enlarging our expanse of heart and fortitude.

When we accept that all things are true, we are not condoning cruelty but enlarging our heart and mind in order to hold it, the way the sky holds a storm to its completion. And in addition to the wisdom we receive for the deepest and longest view of life, we are graced with the comfort and strength of being held by the Eternal Oneness of Heart that has endured and outlived the worst of life on Earth.

This larger perspective enables us to venture into the fallen world with all its travesties and atrocities, not to reframe it or to be defined by it. But to hold it in the oldest part of our being until a deeper logic of Spirit is released by which we can stitch what rips us apart.

There is a profound and disturbing moment in Elie Wiesel's memoir *Night,* which recounts his captivity in Auschwitz. As a fifteen-year-old, he woke one morning to find a boy hanging, dead, in the yard. The silence of his body swaying from the rope had the scent of hell. The older man next to Elie said in disgust, "Where is God?" And, without a thought, young Elie uttered, "In the boy hanging."

This proved to be a spiritual riddle that Elie Wiesel carried with him the rest of his life. As the Jewish philosopher Martin Buber said, "The world is incomprehensible, but it is embraceable." This horrific moment is a compelling example of how all things are true, though not always fair or just. That God is in the boy hanging defies ordinary logic. Only a life of truth and compassion can begin to release the meaning that subsumes this painful moment. Only a life of steadfastness and kindness can remediate the trespasses of human dignity we perpetrate and trip on along the way. In the integral embrace of all life has to offer, we continue, by facing and holding the paradox of being human. In the hope that we can open our hearts one more time than pain closes them.

*Each generation and each life takes its turn in opening
one more time than closing, in giving one more time
than taking, in standing in integrity in the thick of it all.*

## Questions to Walk With

- In your journal, describe your own struggle between love and fear. Then, describe the struggle of our society, as you see it, between love and fear. What choices in your own life and in the life of our society can move us from fear to love?
- In conversation with a friend or loved one, describe something in our time that you find incomprehensible and how you might embrace it to better understand it and move through it.

# The Perennial Choices

> Generosity may be more valuable than stockpiling food, kindness to others more potent than force. These values will determine what world we create, what is born from the ruins.

> —LLEWELLYN VAUGHAN-LEE

WE'VE ALL EXPERIENCED that sudden stretch of highway where one lane is closed due to construction or repair. The electronic arrows are blinking about a mile before everyone is to merge. Traffic is slowing. It's clear that three lanes are going to funnel into one, at least for a time. And sure enough, while most of us start to shuffle our solitary machines into single file, there are always those few who race down the shoulder of the road to the front of the line, ignoring everyone else.

This is a maddening metaphor for the perennial choice between shameless self-interest and self-organizing for the common good. Just as armies simulate battle conditions to train soldiers, lane merging is an occasion to train citizens in the choice-points that enhance or thwart our sense of community.

Haven't we all wanted to stop the scene, get out of our car, and ask the shoulder-racer, "What are you thinking?" Like a dog who eats fast his whole life because he was the runt of the litter, do shoulder-racers dart into every opening, afraid there won't be any space left for them? How do we assure them that if we go at this together, there will be enough for everyone? That's the deeper consideration. How do we begin to teach each other that, at the most fundamental level, self-interest and the common good are one and the same?

The tension between self-interest and the common good intensified during the COVID pandemic. For two years, wearing a mask became a heated symbol for both. Ostensibly, the entire planet was required to wear a mask so as not to unknowingly spread the virus to others. Wearing a mask was, of necessity, an enduring gesture of goodwill. But there was a large contingent, especially in America, who somehow viewed wearing a mask as an infringement on their freedom. This myopic urgency was the epitome of self-interest. It didn't matter how many people might get ill, no one was going to tell them what to do.

As the potter Susan McHenry said, "The viral pandemic revealed a social pandemic that has been festering for decades." And technology has only exacerbated the ways in which we interact and communicate. We are more isolated and, because of that, less trusting. In our modern, global culture, we have become more hidden and more evasive of the full range of our feelings.

The effects of being more isolated and constrained are widespread: from an increase in those who suffer from attention-deficit disorder to an increase in those who suffer from social anxiety to an increase in those who desperately try to feel by cutting themselves or by perpetrating other forms of violence.

Consider the modern plight of dry eyes. In the body's wisdom, we need to tear daily to make sight fluid and possible. However, enough people are experiencing dry eyes for long enough periods of time that it is now considered a medical condition and drugs have been developed to compensate for the loss of tears. TV ads run constantly. But like so many conditions in our society, this only addresses the symptom and not the cause.

In the context of our culture, dry eyes can be seen as another stark manifestation of an emotionally repressed society, in which the need to process and express what we feel is diverted or denied. The pragmatic stoicism of the modern age has been so ingrained in us that our bodies have stopped producing enough tears to lubricate our eyes. This is indicative of an ancient law of consciousness: stop feeling and you stop seeing.

Is it any wonder, then, that our shrinking capacity to feel has been accompanied by a diminishment in the depth and breadth of our vision as a people? That we are gifted in creating more and more sophisticated compensations only blinds us further. As the Hindu thinker Krishnamurti noted, "It is no measure of health to be adjusted to a profoundly sick society."

In an eerie premonition of all this, the existential writer Jean-Paul Sartre imagined, in his classic play *No Exit*, that one of the subtle conditions of living in hell would be that you could never blink, which, only makes seeing drier and more difficult.

There are many inferences we can take from this, but certainly one is that humility has always allowed for the tears that rise from being human to lubricate our eyes. So without feeling and humility, we stumble into a dry, living hell in which numbness and arrogance keep blinding us. These are the cultural currents we have to negotiate and fend off, if we are to find each other and live a life of felt reality which, in turn, enables a life of compassion.

Without compassion lubricating our vision as a people, there is no hope of community or peace. Without access to our feelings, without access to each other, without a belief in the common good, we begin to drift into the currents of evil.

There are two base forms of evil: deliberately and knowingly perpetrating harm and being so dissociated from life that cruelty is found acceptable. And there are two erosions of our humanity that lead to evil: the deadening of our heart and mind and the misperceived need to protect ourselves at all cost from the pain of living, which we insist is coming from everywhere but within ourselves.

Very often, evil is the result of transformations not being allowed to take place. When the risk necessary to feel the pain of true experience is denied, the threshold to wholeness is blocked and that transformational energy is diverted. The focus urgently becomes not feeling the pain of living as we look for the path of least resistance in order to escape the difficulty of living. But when running from life itself, the spiral of our estrangement only deepens.

Once involved in this sort of denial, we are doomed to fend off experience and the world, and in so doing, we quickly become suspect of the actions and motives of others.

However, all that diverted energy will not leave us alone. If we don't engage the risk to feel, we develop stronger means by which to protect ourselves. Then, the avoidance of feeling and conflict escalates into a barricade of stoicism. Without the relief of feeling and connection, the avoidance and fear of life escalate further into paranoia and misanthropy. Then, we are trapped in upholding some principle of survival rather than dealing with the fact that we are running from experience. Sadly, the most insidious form of evil is the self-cruelty that results when we sacralize our avoidance of life.

Like it or not, we are continually challenged to practice staying real. This requires us to keep shedding what is false—from year to year, from self to self. If we can't while in war imagine peace, can't while confused imagine confidence, can't while in fear imagine safety, can't while falling imagine rising—we will lose all sense of hope, which, more than a wanted outcome, is the assurance that we are part of a lasting life-force larger than any one person.

It is from our grounded experience of life that we are compelled to reach out to each other. In Anthony Doerr's brilliant novel *All the Light We Cannot See,* two characters have this exchange during the unfolding of fascism in World War II:

"Then help us."

"I don't want to make trouble, Madame."

"Isn't doing nothing a kind of troublemaking?"

"Doing nothing is doing nothing."

"Doing nothing is as good as collaborating."

"Whom have you put your trust in?"

"You have to trust someone sometime."

Only trust will lead us to authenticity. And only from a place of authenticity can we know real connection. And only from that sense of kinship can we perceive what is possible to repair. Many of us have heard the serenity prayer in which we ask God to give us the power to change that which can be changed and to accept that which cannot be changed, and the wisdom to know the difference. It is a profound guide to finding our way in the world.

But there is a corollary injunction against a sense of false patience that can divert us from facing what needs to be questioned and what needs to be changed. At the height of the Civil Rights Movement, Martin Luther King Jr. articulated as much in his now famous *Letter from Birmingham Jail* when he responded to those who thought his stand for nonviolence insufficient.

He offered this prayer: "If I have said anything that is an overstatement of the truth and is indicative of an unreasonable patience, I beg you to forgive me. If I have said anything that is an understatement of the truth and is indicative of my having patience that makes me [accept] anything less than brotherhood, I beg God forgive me."

At its vital best, community is where we learn to put the common good ahead of our selfishness, to put connection ahead of isolation, and to put feeling ahead of hiddenness. Otherwise, we stall our own development.

As the Canadian theologian Jean Vanier said:

> More and more people are alone. Is it not essential, then, to encourage the creation and growth of places of belonging? If these intermediaries between people and society, these schools of the heart, do not exist, people will find it more and more difficult to achieve maturity.

Yet, for every estrangement that arises from self-interest, there is a story or tradition that affirms the health of the common good. Consider the Kumiai Way that is practiced in Hawaii.

The Japanese word *kumiai* literally translates as "group-join." It now refers to "a volunteer community union." The Kumiai Way invokes a cooperation in times of need, how neighbors offer their talents to help each other during disasters. During such crises, a leaderless and temporary community comes together to meet a particular situation.

Since the 1970s, the ethic of the Kumiai Way has manifest in Hawaii as voluntary neighborhood watch groups, housing subdivision associations, and various ethnic social clubs. Members of the Kumiai Way are expected to be ethical, humble, and committed to act with a cooperative heart.

We face these choices daily: to retreat into self-centered isolation or to be ethical, humble, and committed to act with a cooperative heart. So much depends on whether we view relationships as entangling or liberating. Of course, they can be both. But it is the isolation and avoidance of life that make relationships entangling. And it is our connection and authenticity that make relationships liberating. We teeter between these paths.

All it takes is the opening of a hand or the effort to truly listen to another. These timeless gestures open us to everything. As the iconic songwriter David Byrne said, "Sometimes it's a form of love just to talk to somebody that you have nothing in common with and still be fascinated by their presence."

Each day we wake, get dressed, venture into the world, and face these choices: to deify self-interest or to uphold the common good, to isolate or communicate, to hide from life or face what comes our way, to accept cruelty or enable kindness, to acquiesce to circumstance or to trust the vastness of life, and to thicken our walls or to commit to living with a cooperative heart. In their smallest occurrence, these perennial choices steer us back to each other.

*If we can't while in war imagine peace, can't while confused imagine confidence, can't while in fear imagine safety, can't while falling imagine rising—we will lose all sense of hope.*

## Questions to Walk With

- In your journal, describe one way you practice being real and staying real. How do you know when you need to practice this?
- In conversation with a friend or loved one, describe a time when you were torn between protecting your own self-interest and protecting the common good. When are these the same for you and when are they different?

# The Mind Is an Inlet

IN ESSENCE, THE mind is an inlet, not a container. The mind doesn't author reality. It participates in reality. The mind doesn't create life. It comes alive by joining life. The relationship of our perception to the rest of life opens us to this paradox: to truly be ourselves, we have to learn from everything we are not. A bird is born to nest and fly and so, a bluebird is compelled to enter the sky and not stay in its little house. And salmon are meant to leave their place of birth and return, transforming physiologically along the way. And a caterpillar is meant to spin a cocoon around itself, not to stay there, but to transform in time into a butterfly.

Despite our resistance, the fundamental purpose of perception is to find a way to join everything outside of itself. And so, our long initiation through love and suffering into the humbling and ever-changing life of relationship. In time, we are called to put down our insistence on walls—especially the clear ones we call concepts—and I wouldn't have it any other way.

I recently told a story in one of my teaching circles and I could see that one of my students was troubled by how the story ended. Finally, she said, "I have problems with that story." After a pause, I replied, "I invite you not to *bend* the story to fit your worldview, but to stay in relationship with what jars you about the story until you can *incorporate* it into your worldview." The purpose of perception is not to turn everything into us or into how we already see. Rather, we are meant to grow and not stay self-contained. In this way, the mind is like a dock on the edge of the sea. It is a place of departure into a constantly dynamic vastness in which we baptize ourselves repeatedly.

So, when we encounter something in life that jars us and doesn't fit our pattern of perception, we are challenged not to bend, minimize, or reject it, but to ask of it, "What are you bringing to me that I don't understand?"

By default, we often misuse our mind and make it a self-replicating machine until we walk about the world as a descendant of Midas. But instead of turning everything we touch into gold, we turn everything we touch into some mirrored aspect of ourselves. Until, as D. H. Lawrence laments in his poem "New Heaven and Earth:"

> I shall never forget the maniacal horror of it all in the end
> when everything was me . . . I kissed the woman I loved,
> and God of horror, I was kissing also myself.

To let in only what matches what we think and only what we have already felt sorely limits the scope and depth of our compassion. When we lost our beloved yellow lab Mira, we were sent cascading into an unprecedented tumble of grief. And there were those who couldn't understand such grief for a dog. They refused to let their perception join with life outside of their guarded experience. When I almost died of cancer in my thirties, there were those so afraid of their own death that they refused to let in the inevitability of death. As if the moat of ignorance could protect them from death.

The greatest misuse of the mind is when we make it self-referential because that insidious solipsism puts a clear film of self-consciousness around us, which prevents us from being touched by other life. Through the bubble of solipsism, we unravel all experience of otherness into a projected image of our own thinking. Honestly, this is absurd in the original sense of the word, which comes from the Latin *absurdus,* meaning "deaf" or "out of tune."

All we have to do to remind ourselves that life is more than our own perception is stand on a hill full face to the wind. Then, once again, it is clear, we did not create the wind. And once again, we are reminded that a deep purpose of our will is to climb into the open. And an enduring purpose of experience is to put our face into the wind, letting that unseeable force refresh our mind.

Ultimately, we are always being called to lean into what is beyond us, asking in earnest, "Fill me with life and teach me what I don't know." For giving into the sea that surrounds it, the shell is rounded until it reveals its inner beauty. Likewise, the mind at its best is a humble shell being scoured by the vast ocean of life until it is rounded enough to reveal its inner beauty. There is no quieter or greater destiny than to be thoroughly alive inside and out. It's how the bluebird brings the sky back into its tiny house. And how the salmon returns to the site of its birth completely transformed in time to die. And how one self undoes itself into the next the way a caterpillar transforms unthinkably into a butterfly.

As the Romantic poet Shelley puts it: "The mind in creation is as a fading coal, which some invisible influence, like an inconstant wind, awakens to transitory brightness." And so we flare and fade, coming alive and lighting the things around us until in turn, we are lighted. For try as we will, no amount of self-imitation or enshrining of what we already know will solidify our worth. We awaken our worth when rushed through by life, the way an inlet is brought alive by the rush of water sluicing through it.

*The fundamental purpose of perception is to find a way to join everything outside of itself.*

## Questions to Walk With

- In your journal, describe a time when you encountered something outside of your current way of thinking that jarred you. How did you respond? Did you bend, minimize, or reject this new knowledge or did you stay in conversation with it? How did this newness impact you?

- In conversation with a friend or loved one, describe something that is currently new to your manner of perception and how it is challenging you. Discuss how you might relate to this new way of knowing going forward.

# To Look or Not to Look

THERE IS AN ancient Greek myth that carries within it, like a message in a bottle, one of the most crucial struggles we face as living beings. It is the story of a gifted musician, Orpheus, whose love, Eurydice, is taken by Hades, the god of the underworld. Orpheus is so grief-stricken that he travels to the land of the dead to plead with Hades to give Eurydice back. After a cold and deliberate consideration, Hades says, "You can have her. It will take you three days to bring her back to the land of the living. There is one condition. You must carry her and you must *not* look at her face until you reach the light. If you do, she will return to me forever."

Unfortunately, unknown to Orpheus, Hades tells Eurydice the opposite: "He will carry you to the land of the living, and you *must* look at him before you reach the light. If you do *not,* you will return to me forever." Their colossal struggle fails and Eurydice is lost forever.

The struggle for us, though, is ongoing. For there is an Orpheus in each of us that believes, *if I look, I will die.* There is also a Eurydice in each of us that believes, *if I don't look, I will die.* And so, the great spiritual question after *to be or not to be* is *to look or not to look.* The personal balance we arrive at determines whether we make it out of Hell or not.

Though it shifts throughout our lives, according to our struggles and devotions, each of us is born with a natural leaning toward looking or not looking. Not surprisingly, I am one of those feminine seers, for I believe that if I don't look, I will die. This probably has a lot to do with my calling to be a poet.

But, like each of us, I wrestle with both tendencies: to be the keeper of secrets or the discoverer of truths. Though no one can tell us how, we have to work this great battle between looking and not looking, again and again, in order to leave the underworld and make our way back into the land of the living.

More deeply, each of these inclinations—to look or not to look—has its proper domain. Similar to the Chinese notions of yin and yang, which represent the receptive and active forces in the Universe, we forever open and close as we look or not into what life brings us. It is not by accident that the receptive, feminine quality in each of us believes we must look if we are to know what is true, while the active, masculine quality in each of us believes we must not look too long if we aim to keep moving forward. Neither impulse unto itself is detrimental. At their best, these impulses complement each other, allowing us to fully comprehend what matters while showing us how to act in the world in order to bring what matters into being.

The challenge is to understand how these inclinations live in us and not to indulge them so much that they get the better of us. To not look when you know you have to fuels the life of fear. Imagine the proverbial boogeyman in the closet. The more we don't look, the larger and more frightening that goblin becomes. Yet, once we summon the courage to look, the fear dissipates and the darkness of the closet seems to dissipate as well. But the quality of light in the closet doesn't actually change at all. It is our eyes that grow accustomed to the dark, which allows us to *see* more clearly into the closet. When we have the courage to look, we can outwait the fear we carry and *see* into the dark.

Carl Jung said, "Neurosis is the substitute for legitimate suffering." And not looking when you know you have to creates the pain of neurosis, the pain of not facing things, the pain of maintaining our denial of what life is bringing forward.

On the other hand, to look when you know you mustn't fuels the life of doubt and worry. If I am troubled and pained by something you said that was hurtful, I can replay it in my mind a dozen times—thinking one more iteration will make me feel better. But it never works. At least, that is my experience. For looking again and again when you know you mustn't is at the obsessive heart of worry. Going over things repeatedly—over-analyzing, over-questioning—creates a false sense of control that only throws us deeper into doubt and worry.

This is the cautionary tale of Hamlet who, knowing he must act to invoke justice for his father's murder, revisits every decision before him so many times that he unravels his certainty about everything. This over-analyzing leaves him enervated and full of painful doubt, even about his very existence.

When pulled so forcefully into ruminating on our experience (by going over what happened, by revisiting what was said or what was done, again and again), the only way out is to drop it—precisely at the moment it feels impossible to drop. This is a necessary practice, if we are to regain our place in the world.

A great teacher about this for me surfaced in a poem of mine, called "Practicing," which goes like this:

> As a man in his last breath
> drops all he is carrying
>
> each breath is a little death
> that can set us free.

How we discern when to look and when not to look is a lifelong practice of self-awareness. Otherwise, the tenuous nature of life can inflate our fear and the weight of too much thought can deepen our worry and doubt.

Ultimately, while we need both capacities to live fully, we need the courage to look more often than the discipline not to. Just as a flower must keep opening for there to be spring, we must look and not turn away. And just as a wave must keep cresting for the sea to keep reaching the shore, we must lean ever more into life.

> *The great spiritual question after to be or*
> *not to be is to look or not to look.*

## Questions to Walk With ══════════════

- Describe one thing you need to look at that you are avoiding. What small step can you take to look in that place in order to minimize the life of your fear?

- In conversation with a friend or loved one, describe one thing you need to stop looking at in order to minimize the life of your worry. What small step can you take not to look in that place anymore?

- In conversation with a friend or loved one, discuss which you are more inclined to do: look or not look at what life brings your way. How has this basic position of perception helped or hurt you?

# Uncharted Waters

BEN IS A student in a yearlong journey I offer. He is sensitive, thoughtful, humble, and completely present, a deep listener who is always putting things together. During our last gathering, Ben revealed that he served as a US Navy submarine officer of the deck and nuclear engineer during the Cold War, and was later deployed to the Middle East as the second in charge of a battalion of US Navy Seabees in support of Operation Iraqi Freedom. He described those worlds as absolute and black and white. With no room for error, there is an immense reliance on training and meticulous preparation. Every action and decision is checked numerous times for strict compliance with governing principles.

Ben went on to explain that listening underwater through passive sonar is how you "see" in a submarine. But if you approach uncharted waters, you must avoid that terrain. For running blind, you could hit silent unknown reefs or seamounts and cause catastrophic damage. Ben paused and softened even further. Then, he said, "Such an absolute way was appropriate for that time and that work. But I started to question if such a devotion to perfection was useful in living the rest of my life. And this is what led me into the kind of inner work we're doing together."

Ben's insight is a compelling example of a turning point in our journey that everyone faces sooner or later. For where and how we are introduced to our gifts is not always where we are called to use them. We can grow entrenched and attached to the circumstances of our learning and struggle when challenged to use our gifts in a different way. You may learn how to use a hammer and a screwdriver by taking things apart, only to realize that you are meant to apply these skills in putting things together.

In Ben's case, he could easily have stayed committed to an absolute life, seeking perfection in his sense of self and his relationships with no tolerance for mistakes or mishaps. Many of us are plagued by the desire to be perfect and live in the painful gap between who we aspire to be and who we actually are—fearing our life will explode if we make a mistake.

Yet something in Ben—perhaps the light of his soul or his authority of being—knew that the only way to truly grow into our aliveness is to *enter* uncharted waters, not avoid them. And when we can listen deeply, our heart is the sonar by which we can navigate uncharted waters. It is the most sensitive and far-reaching of all inner instruments.

Thus, the need to become conversant and skilled in reading the heart and how it tells us to move forward with integrity. It is interesting that the naval instruction for an underwater mission is "run silent, run deep"—invoked to avoid being discovered as a target. This mantra also applies to the inner mission we are called to enter as we move through the depth of the spiritual journey. Inwardly, we must "run silent, run deep" in order to discover who we are.

All this is complicated in the modern world by the exponential reach of technology. For while our reach multiplies to the moon and beyond, the life of our care remains additive—one moment of care on Earth adding to the next.

For all its gifts, technology has caused us to outreach our heart. And so, there is a gap that can only be filled by the work we do to inhabit an inner life. It helps to remember that our arms grow directly out of our heart. This is why integrity can be measured by how much of what we know to be true informs what we do. This is how our goodness is known, by how much of our heart reaches the world through the authentic mark of our hands. Only care, kindness, compassion, and wonder will help lessen the gap between our technology and our heart. Our challenge is to constantly reduce the gap between our care and our reach.

*The only way to truly grow into our aliveness is*
*to enter uncharted waters, not avoid them.*

## Questions to Walk With

- In your journal, describe a growing edge that represents uncharted waters for you and how you are called to enter those waters and how you are avoiding them. Describe one step you can take to enter those waters.

# Here and There

ONE OF THE most insidious conditions to plague us as human beings is the assumption that life is happening other than where we are. Certainly, there are infinite aspects of life all happening at once. While you're reading this, millions of souls around the world are experiencing their own facets of Now: sleeping, waking, dying, being born, falling in love, falling out of love, breaking, healing, finding a dream, and, at once, watching a dream fall apart. But when in pain or flooded with fear or weighed down with a lack of worth, we imagine that a more valuable version of life is just out of reach—over there. And then, we stop inquiring into the life we have. We stop inhabiting the one life we're given.

The timeless secret that I was opened to by almost dying of cancer in my thirties is that there is no there. There is only here. The paradox at the heart of the Mystery of Life is that through living the Eternal Now that is before us, we can glimpse and feel and access the Eternal Now that everyone is experiencing everywhere at once, if we can stay authentic and true to our own experience.

For many years, I have been blessed to convene circles and journey with kind souls everywhere I go. And one sweet paradox that I experience over and over is that I travel all over the world only, once there, to affirm to everyone that there is nowhere to go. And I'm happy to do it. It is a privilege. Of course, we all travel from many different places to gather, but once together, that space always opens to the same Eternal Moment—the same Here.

Years ago, I would visit a small lake in the Adirondacks during the summer. The far side of the lake was state land and so remained undeveloped. I would get up early and have coffee on our dock and watch the sun coat the far shore, which seemed so mystical in its aura of simplicity. By the third morning of this particular summer, I felt compelled to sit on that farther shore, as if life's secret was waiting there. I had to get there. So I placed my coffee in the bottom of the small boat and rowed to the other side. After twenty minutes of rowing, I nudged the hull upon the stone beach, got my coffee, and sat in the very spot I had been drawn to. I sighed and looked back across the way. And sure enough, where I had been sitting on our dock, now seemed so mystical in its aura of simplicity. I laughed to understand that there is no there—only here.

A few years ago, I had a follow-up lesson around all this. I was up early at a rural retreat center. It was spring and I was taking a walk before we got started for the day. There was a sheen and glare on the far hill that drew me like the Adirondack shore. As I walked toward the hill, I was struck by how beautiful it was, gleaming in its totality, uplifted in the early sun. As I walked closer, the details of the hill started to come into focus. There was a dead tree with an eaten-out stump and remnants of a wire fence were tangled in the high grass. As I reached the hill itself, I could see on the far side the carcass of a deer. The closer I got, the more I could see the reality of the hill below the glare. And the hill was saying without words that the challenge, for all of us, is to see below the glare and love what is there anyway.

This speaks to the difference between falling in love and being in love. Initially, we are drawn to each other like far-off hills radiating in our glare of possibility. My god, how beautiful. I want to get closer. I want to go there, even live there. Then, as we get closer, the reality of a life lived shows itself below the glare. But often, the one approaching will say, "You didn't tell me about this dead, eaten-out tree. And what about this wire fence? And you never mentioned the dead deer.

Why are you hiding these things?" And the one being approached is hurt and replies, "I am hiding nothing. Can't you love me as I am?"

In this relational space, "there" is equivalent to what we imagine others to be or want them to become and "here" is accepting others for who they are. And the challenge, when drawn into love, is to see below the glare of what we want our loved one to be and love them in all their messy detail. In this, we are asked repeatedly to leave the ideal behind for what is real—in life as well as in relationship. A seminal expression about all this is Shakespeare's "Sonnet 130."

In Elizabethan times, the object of courtly love was the ideal. And so, poets of the day pined for the ideal and praised their loves as radiant and perfect. Shakespeare was no different in the beginning and his first 129 sonnets conform to the elevated description of the romantic ideal. Then, Shakespeare was broken from his trance with the glare of perfect love. No one knows what happened but "Sonnet 130" veers completely from the pursuit of the ideal to celebrate, almost crudely, the more lasting love of what is real:

> My mistress' eyes are nothing like the sun;
> Coral is far more red than her lips' red;
> If snow be white, why then her breasts are dun;
> If hairs be wires, black wires grow on her head.
> I have seen roses damasked, red and white,
> But no such roses see I in her cheeks;
> And in some perfumes is there more delight
> Than in the breath that from my mistress reeks.
> I love to hear her speak, yet well I know
> That music hath a far more pleasing sound;
> I grant I never saw a goddess go;
> My mistress when she walks treads on the ground.
> And yet, by heaven, I think my love as rare
> As any she belied with false compare.

This description of his love would be cruel, if not for the last two lines. For Shakespeare grounds his love in the real almost to a flaw.

And yet, he says that his love is as rare—in her full humanness—as any love she falsely compares herself to in her insecurity. He sees her earthly traits and failings and loves her anyway—beneath the glare of her possibility.

While Shakespeare is extreme to make a point, it is the face of our ordinary being as we move through the world that is most loveable, when we can accept that there is nowhere to go but here. And I confess, the more I've removed between my heart and the world, the more I'm able to love things as they are with all their markings of time. It's how a broken bit of glass in an alley reflecting the sun is as precious as a wildflower opening on the edge of a forest.

Our need to see things as they are and love what's there is central to our experience of peace and eventually joy. Yet how do we practice this? Perhaps by giving our heart's attention completely to what is before us until it reveals its lasting beauty in its worn and broken detail. We're on the edge of winter as I write this and the bare trees are showing all their cuts and breaks from earlier storms. They can hide nothing in the gray December afternoons. Their bareness has a beauty all its own in the same way that a life well-lived shows all its scars and limitations, even more worthy of love for having lived so much.

As a young sculptor, Auguste Rodin, having no money to hire a beautiful model, wound up paying an elderly handyman with a broken nose to pose for him. This led him to realize that lasting beauty is not just in the glare of what is pleasant and welcoming but more so in the lived and weathered endurance of our presence over time.

And the early Chinese sage Seng-Ts'an said, "There is no here, no there; / infinity is right before your eyes." Life is happening everywhere at once, even though we say that wherever we are is here and wherever we are not is there. But everywhere is Now. While it helps to break up Oneness in order to comprehend what is incomprehensible, we quickly forget that it is our limitations that make the breaking up of Oneness necessary.

For, just as someone starving can't eat a whole loaf of bread at once, the conscious heart must live off small pieces of Infinity in order to digest what will nourish us. Still, the blind know that the world is seeable beyond their darkness and the deaf know that the world is full of music beyond their silence. Only the mind in its stubbornness can insist that the world is defined by what it can take in.

The sheen and glare of life as we meet it is not a promise of more but a doorway to what is lasting and real, when we can move through our expectations and ideals. After all, you can't live in the glare, you can only outlast it. The question is whether you will be disappointed once the glare disperses or realize you are Here and that it is our home.

> *The challenge, for all of us, is to see below*
> *the glare and love what is there anyway.*

## Questions to Walk With

- Describe a time when you thought life or love was other than where you were. How did this affect you? Where are you living mostly now—Here or There?

# Building What Can Serve

———

> The purpose of all the major religious traditions is not to
> construct big temples on the outside, but to create temples
> of goodness and compassion inside, in our hearts.
>
> —Dalai Lama

THIS SECTION EXPLORES the resources that will help us:

- work together to repair our impassable roads and to find or
  create new ones.

Heaven is within us and inside every moment. We can reach
it through our authenticity and vulnerability, if we have the
courage not to run when opened to that depth by love or suffering. This practice of building what can serve is the enduring
covenant we make with life, when we commit to being awake
and to inhabiting a life of care. Practicing Heaven requires our
presence, listening, and tending. These elemental vows restore
our direct experience of life, which animates our sense of how
rare it is to be alive at all. From that awakened threshold, we
can find each other and experience the sensation of Oneness,
which is joy. The chapters in this section explore the ways we can
practice heaven, including how we keep coming alive by tending to each other, how the true purpose of memory is to help us

reconstitute the Whole, how learning is always there to help us repair, how life is nothing less than an honest classroom, how we drift between fear and welcome, and what it means to walk with wonder in the world.

# Here Abide

Oh how could heaven be anywhere but here?
Stay true to the actual, yielding to all things . . .

—T'ao Ch'ien

For years I have coached all the youngins against despair. Now, the wheel has turned again, and the cities are burning, and the old look for God while the lost know they are here by how much they hurt. And though my mind keeps healing like a cracked rib, I still have this trust that the inlet we call life brings in much more than muck.

I am born of another dark time that few want to speak of. And yet, I feel an enduring tie to the wonders and sorrows of being Jewish. For genocides like the Holocaust are psychic tsunamis that affect us generations on. So, I remain awash in the heartbreak and awe of the Jewish soul and the long trail of our strength and suffering. I remain a student of all those who have endured without becoming what oppressed them. In endurance with kindness, we abide.

The name Poland is believed to have come from the Hebrew words *po lin* which mean "here abide." Legend has it that these words were inscribed on a note descended from Heaven and found by refugees leaving Germany during the massacre of Jews during the middle ages. And now, the instruction falls to us, "Here abide."

*Abide,* from the Old English root "onward," means "to accept or live in accordance with." So, "here abide" suggests that we move on in accord with life by accepting the light that shows itself through the storms we encounter. "To abide here" means that we face adversity by moving through it, that onward doesn't mean to leave but to live here more deeply. "To abide here" demands that we reach through the storm to the depth that is unaffected by it, that we outlast the turbulence to uncover the calm.

It has taken seventy-seven years but, in Germany today, it's illegal to place a worker in a room without a window. This is law. This seems a ripple of cultural repair, offering a semblance of peace after the apocalypse of World War II in which millions were herded like cattle into boxcars with no windows or air.

The legendary psychiatrist Viktor Frankl, who survived several concentration camps, once recommended that the Statue of Liberty on the East Coast of the United States be complemented by a Statue of Responsibility on the West Coast:

> Freedom is only part of the story and half of the truth. Freedom is but the negative aspect of the whole phenomenon whose positive aspect is responsibleness. In fact, freedom is in danger of degenerating into mere arbitrariness unless it is lived in terms of responsibleness. That is why I recommend that the Statue of Liberty on the East Coast be supplemented by a Statue of Responsibility on the West Coast.

Crucial to any sense of abidance is our relentless effort to be responsive to all that befalls us. Just as kindness begins with the smallest gesture (the lifting of a heavy load or the dab of a cloth to a weary friend's brow), cruelty also begins with the smallest twist (the exclusion of a foreigner or the hiding of someone's glasses). So, we have to cooperate with life and not fight it. We have to find our worth in working with and not against. We have to be responsive and hold nothing back in how we give and how we receive.

Whether we are facing personal crises or social tragedies, these sustaining questions remain: How do we practice enduring without becoming what oppresses us? How do we outlast the turbulence to uncover the calm? How do we endure with kindness? How do we "here abide" and live in accordance with the more lasting elements that sustain us?

And while courage is necessary, it is not something we summon by ourselves alone. Courage is a force we cooperate with in order to release. Much like a bird's effort to glide on the wind. Though flight seems impossible from the ground, once in the air, the bird is required to open its wings, lift, pump, and find the current of wind, to which it surrenders.

It's important to note that a bird can't open its wings fully without exposing its chest. So, a bird can't fly without leading with its heart. The human equivalent is our commitment to saying yes to life. Saying yes to life is how effort finds grace. Courage begins, as Mother Teresa said, "by doing small things with love." To care is how we open our wings and love is the wind we surrender to.

Still, we will inevitably be challenged by the smallness of others when their fear and stinginess of heart violate our boundaries. But this progression, if leaned into, will offer us the chance to stand in integrity, not giving people who imagine power over us any sort of foothold.

In facing such a challenge, you become an unexpected model of steadfastness. Then, without your knowing, you give me strength to further be myself. Then, when fear makes me small and stingy, it is the strength of your kindness and truth that helps me reclaim the fullness of my heart. This is all part of the relational journey. No one is exempt.

We all face small choices that have big consequences. A cruel indifference can lead to agitation and anxiety, while a small kindness can lead to a sense of foundation and a depth of peace.

Just yesterday, I was renewed by the laughter of a child and stirred to help a stranger who had trouble at their door. With nothing to show for it, these efforts made me more whole. You see, at times, we stumble into grace. When searching for a way, what lasts can appear when a sudden rain washes the worry from my mind. When confused or lost, what matters can seep like light through a cloud into the heart of someone ready to begin again. To be so renewed, to stumble into grace—this, too, is what it means to abide.

Perhaps peace will come again, the way spring follows winter, when more of us turn to tears than not, till the water of all tribes forms a river in which those with guns will wash the blood from their faces and rise unsure of what they've done.

As for me, I have looked in our time and throughout history for models of worthiness and have found many who are true and heroic. But the most inspiring are so uniquely themselves that I am left with the diaspora of myself. For no one can show me how to abide, though I am encouraged by all. I only know that kindness is the currency we give away in order to become whole.

*"To abide here" demands that we reach through
the storm to the depth that is unaffected by it, that
we outlast the turbulence to uncover the calm.*

## Questions to Walk With

- In order to glide, a bird is required to open its wings, lift, pump, and find the current of wind, to which it surrenders. This is equivalent to our process in cooperating with courage. In your journal, explore what it means for you to open your heart, to lift yourself up, to find the larger current of life, and to then surrender so you can be carried by courage. Describe each part of this process personally and, later, detail what next steps in each of these areas might look like for you.
- In conversation with a friend or loved one, describe the markers of authenticity by which you know you are on course in your life.

# The Purpose of Memory

If you can see a thing whole . . . it seems that it's always beautiful.

—Ursula Le Guin

In *More Together Than Alone*, I wrote about a museum in Indonesia where an early statue of Kuan Yin was discovered and put on exhibit. The ancient statue became an enormous attraction, not just with tourists but with the people living there. Large crowds would stay for hours, ignoring the velvet ropes and the decorum of the museum. Some would chant. Others would dance. And others began throwing petals at the feet of Kuan Yin. What was retrieved and put on exhibit as an example of something that was sacred in the past was very much alive and a current shrine for prayer. For the villagers, the statue of Kuan Yin was not an artifact but a living deity. And so, when Kuan Yin came alive, the museum stopped being a museum and the curators were challenged to question their very purpose.

While museums and libraries serve as wellsprings for every generation to preserve what is meaningful and sacred, the deeper purpose of memory is not just to preserve the past but to care for things that have mattered until they can come alive again.

This in turn necessitates an ongoing awareness by which we can discern when things that matter come alive again. This is crucial to our evolution of spirit, because living things require different forms of care than preserving things that were alive.

Consider a museum that is preserving an old oil painting of a flower. The room is kept dark and cool to preserve the ancient brushstrokes and remnants of paint. But what if the flower were to mysteriously come alive; don't we then have to let the light in and water the flower? Don't we have to care for what comes alive in a more immediate and nurturing way? This is the difference between deifying the past through nostalgia and letting the past help us live into the future. Recognizing when things come alive and changing our sense of care is part of our heartwork as a human being.

When my father died, I took a few of his tools, and now I have them on my desk. It is an exhibit in my personal museum. One of those tools is an awl. Its red wooden handle is chipped and slightly warped. Seeing his tool on my desk helps me feel his presence and impact on my life. But last summer, we needed to build new pottery shelves for my wife, Susan. And I needed an awl. Suddenly, my father's tool was in my hand, building again. I was holding the handle he held, pressing my palm where he had pressed his. It felt like we were building something together. After the shelves were done, I put the awl back on my desk where it glows in an entirely deeper way.

There is nothing wrong with museums or with personal collections of objects that have meaning for us. What is crucial is that we preserve things that have meaning and stay open to when they will come alive again.

Yet, trauma represents a type of memory that we don't want to come alive again. We actually want trauma to loosen its grip, so the past doesn't script our behavior in the future. This requires a different kind of heartwork.

The power of the past is everywhere and is not to be underestimated. Recently, Susan finished throwing a bowl and left it in the damp room to set before firing. When she returned a few days later, someone had knocked her bowl before it set and the rim was slightly warped. The bowl was still wet enough that Susan was able to reshape the rim. The bowl finally set and was fired, but when it came out of the kiln, the rim had returned to its warped state. Susan was puzzled when the oldest potter, the one she considers a quiet master, appeared behind her, "Oh, this happens from time to time. Once in the fire, a broken pot can keep the memory of its break."

Often, the memory of the break returns in our mind and in our heart. With such deep wounds and scars, we can look to trees for instruction. A tree that has been cut or broken simply takes its time in growing around the cut or break. It lets its growth incorporate the scar until it becomes part of the face of the tree. Hard as it is to practice, one of the most enduring responses we can have to trauma is to grow around the scar until it is no longer a dominant feature in our life. Though I believe this to be true, I still struggle in living this out.

Being human, we are challenged constantly to care for things in memory until they can come alive again and help us live *and,* with all things traumatic, we are challenged *not* to keep the painful things alive that will keep us from living anew. We each need to develop our own personal practice in working with the true purpose of memory. In time, I have found that the more authentic and vulnerable I can stay in living my life, the more the relics in my personal museum leave their exhibits, freeing up more space in my heart for what is yet to come.

> *The deeper purpose of memory is not just to*
> *preserve the past but to care for things that have*
> *mattered until they can come alive again.*

## Questions to Walk With

- In your journal, describe a painful time from which the memory of the break keeps returning to your mind and heart. Now, practice enlarging your life by inhaling the rest of you around this break. Do this daily for a week and journal about the experience.
- In conversation with a friend or loved one, describe one object in your personal museum that is waiting to come alive to be used

now, one thing in your museum that is a live resource waiting to help you. Later, if the resource is nearby, take it in your hand. If it is not available, create a symbol for it and take that in your hand. Breathe in the living power of this resource. Do this daily for a week and journal about the experience.

# Keeper of the Tablets

If you have a garden and a library, you have everything you need.

—Cicero

As a child, I received a library card as soon as I could sign my name. I was four or five at the time, and my brother and I drove my mother crazy, taking out what seemed like enormous books, forcing her to read to us while gazing in amazement at pictures larger than our heads. The sense of discovery was tremendous and caused me to realize, early on, that there was a world beyond me. Even before I could read, I tapped into the mystery of the written page, and books loomed as magical portals which drew me. I was never far from them.

I grew up near the sea and my first true sense of solitude came when sitting in the bow of our boat, watching the endless waves reflect and go clear as they swelled and passed. My other lasting sense of solitude came in the presence of the books on my shelves. And now, it's hard to separate the two. For going where books take you, either in the writing or the reading, is so much like sailing out to sea. Being alone in our reflection is like being alone in the bow of a boat. In both instances, the world reflects in your face until suddenly, in a moment of clarity, you can see on through to the bottom of things.

Even now, there are stacks of books about my bed, which I open like willing friends, moving among them freely, reading and rereading passages that connect me to all that is essential. When I discovered I was a poet, the poetry shelves became a sanctuary where I heard soulful voices for the first time, a time-traveling oasis where I tried on many selves. As I grew in my own sense of consciousness, I found spirits there that understood, and frames of mind that made me feel less solitary. It was a secret camaraderie—steering my turbulent, adolescent heart through the honest currents of Rainer Maria Rilke, Hermann Hesse, Pablo Neruda, William Carlos Williams, Adrienne Rich, Robert Penn Warren, Muriel Rukeyser, Longinus, and Plato. I felt spacious in their presence and verified in a way of life I barely knew.

In trying to understand the nature of writing, I was drawn to why libraries began, and discovered, not surprisingly, that the life of a writer and the life of what's written have a great deal in common. While writing developed as a means to express and integrate the essence of human experience, libraries began as a means to link those experiences and preserve that essence.

Since the beginning of time, libraries and those who preserve knowledge and ways of knowing have created a lineage. The word *library* comes from the Latin *librarium,* meaning "chest for books," and from *liber,* meaning "the inner bark of trees." Implicit in the original sense of the word is the notion that libraries preserve the inner bark of humanity.

The first libraries date back to 3500 BC. They were composed, for the most part, of published records. Excavations from the ancient cities of Sumer, located in southern Iraq, revealed temple rooms full of clay tablets in cuneiform. At Nineveh, archaeologists discovered over thirty thousand clay tablets from the Library of Ashurbanipal, dating back to the eighth century BC.

Early Chinese libraries began with the Qin dynasty, where the library catalog was written on fine silk scrolls and stored in silk bags. Yet it wasn't until the eighth century AD that the Arab world began to import the craft of papermaking from China. One of the first paper mills was at work in Baghdad in 794. By the ninth century AD, public libraries started to appear in many Islamic cities.

In 983 in Shiraz, Adud al-Dawlah created a magnificent library, described by the medieval historian al-Muqaddasi as "a complex of buildings surrounded by gardens with lakes and waterways. The buildings were topped with domes, and comprised an upper and lower story with a total of 360 rooms. In each department, catalogues were placed on a shelf and the rooms were furnished with carpets."

But it was Johannes Gutenberg's startling discovery of movable type in the 1400s that revolutionized bookmaking and the burgeoning of modern libraries. In 1571, based on his own extensive collection, Cosimo de' Medici completed the Laurentian Library in Florence, Italy, famous as a repository for more than eleven thousand manuscripts and 4,500 printed books. The earliest example in England of a truly public library was the Francis Trigge Chained Library in Grantham, Lincolnshire, established in 1598.

The American Library of Congress was established on April 24, 1800, when President John Adams signed an Act of Congress transferring the seat of government from Philadelphia to the new capital of Washington, DC. Part of the legislation appropriated five thousand dollars "for the purchase of such books as may be necessary for the use of Congress and for fitting up a suitable apartment for containing them." Books were ordered from London, and the collection, consisting of 740 books and thirty maps, was housed in the new Capitol.

The fledgling Library of Congress was destroyed in August 1814, when invading British troops set fire to the Capitol Building and its small library of three thousand volumes. Within a month, former president Thomas Jefferson offered his personal library as a replacement. Jefferson had spent fifty years accumulating a wide variety of books, including many in foreign languages, and volumes of philosophy, science, and literature. In January 1815, Congress accepted Jefferson's offer, appropriating $23,950 for his 6,487 books.

Today, the Library of Congress includes more than thirty-two million cataloged books and other print materials in 470 languages; more than sixty-one million manuscripts; one million issues of world newspapers spanning the past three centuries; 4.8 million maps; 2.7 million sound recordings; and more than 13.7 million prints and photographic images.

This overview is just a glimpse of our human need to preserve and evolve our many ways of knowing. The truth is that human beings have tried to write on everything including leaves, bark, the hides of animals, clay, wood, stone, and metal. We have also tried to write with everything from sticks to bones to feathers. And in an age where software packages rhyme for us, we still need to write without any filters in order to find our place in Eternity.

My deepest attempt to render Eternity came during the time I was working on my epic poem *Fire Without Witness*. During the six years it took to research that book, I tented in many libraries like a nomad en route to some promised land, taking clues and souvenirs with me. The four hundred pages of details and quotes that I discovered became the palette from which I painted my epic poem. I was intoxicated with the plot lines of history and with bringing them alive. I must say that the experience of research brought me alive. This deep journey of inquiry would not have been possible without the life of libraries. Without access to this flood of books, I would have been trapped in my own time, trapped in my own perception of things, and trapped in the current age without access to the human lineage.

When *Fire Without Witness* was published, I quietly went to my hometown library, looking for those enormous books I held as a child. They were all lost, of course, but I found my own on a shelf, which I couldn't reach as a boy. I stood there and thought of those clay tablets in the early Library of Ashurbanipal found in Nineveh. I felt humbled to add my scratch marks to the pile.

And now, as social media augments the erosion of precise language day by day, the role of librarians as guardians of human inquiry grows even more indispensable. It is compelling that in our libraries, cultures and thinkers of every faith live side by side in better harmony and tolerance than we can manage around the globe. The modern astronomer Carl Sagan declared that "the health of our civilization, the depth of our awareness about the underpinnings of our culture, and our concern for the future can all be tested by how well we support our libraries."

When I think of the peace that resides in the fact that libraries exist, I'm reminded that one of the earliest librarians was a Babylonian named Amit Anu who was known as "Keeper of the Tablets" in the Royal Library at Ur nearly four thousand years ago. He was a scribe who was an elder.

Books are still necessary and everyone who preserves them and cares for them is a "Keeper of the Tablets," descendants of this noble yet invisible profession of being guardians of what we know and how we know. Without such guardians, as William Butler Yeats has warned, "The center cannot hold."

*While writing developed as a means to express and integrate the essence of human experience, libraries began as a means to link those experiences and preserve that essence.*

## Questions to Walk With

- In your journal, enter an imaginary conversation with an ancient librarian and tell the story of the most treasured book in that library and how that library came into being.
- In conversation with a friend or loved one, tell the story of someone you admire who loves books and how you came to know this about them. What is it that they love about books?
- In your journal, describe a time when you were opened to a new world through a book. How did you come upon this book? How did this journey of learning change you?

# The Honest Classroom

The sanctity of true inquiry has a long history and can be found in the ancient, informal gatherings of Buddha, Confucius, Jesus, and Socrates, as well as in the modern classrooms of Pema Chodron, Jack Kornfield, Tara Brach, and Joan Halifax. The heart of all the great teachings is that we learn by inquiring into the nature of things, as well as into the nature of each other, and ultimately, by inquiring into our relationship with the Whole.

The French philosopher Rabelais said, "A child is a fire to be lit, not a vase to be filled." The premise is that each of us is complete to begin with. We only need to have our filament of Wholeness ignited.

One of William Blake's proverbs reads, "Straight are the roads to improvement, but crooked are the roads to Genius." While course corrections can help us better navigate the world, the unexpected meanderings, the explorations that can't be foreseen, are the questions that spark us and lead us into moments of enlightenment. True wisdom lies beyond all plans.

Likewise, the honest classroom discovers a wisdom beyond all intent. The teachers who do nothing but correct their students presume to know what is right for everyone, and, indeed, already have the answers in place before the questions are ever asked. Such a teacher, such a vase-filler, already knows the destination. The teacher who encourages discovery is on a journey, too. This teacher is willing to learn from students, and so, precludes nothing.

The bedrock of true inquiry is to treat everything and everyone before you as an equal. This commitment to equality is the foundation of any classroom, if true learning is to take place. Humble, open-hearted teachers can respect their students as peers. This creates a safe and common place where questions can be asked and risks can be taken.

In order to do this, the classroom needs to become an unconditional forum. This means that the concept of right and wrong does not pertain to an individual's feelings and opinions. Unconditional acceptance, however, does not preclude feedback or criticism, but focuses such energy on the accuracy of one's efforts and not the validity of one's view. To be kind and honest, and unconditional and constructive, are not mutually exclusive. It requires diligence and compassion from everyone involved.

Yet how does an honest classroom maintain its safety and integrity? It depends on the integrity and compassion of the teacher, who is the one in the room asking the most questions and taking the most risks. An educational setting can only be as truthful as the teacher who leads it, only as real as the teacher who inhabits it, only transformative to the degree that the teacher is willing to be transformed.

To truly teach is far more than the retention and distribution of knowledge. It requires the inner resources of the person teaching. In order to nurture the discovery of Wholeness, whether through physics or art history, the person teaching must invest their full humanity in an effort to release the depth of meaning inherent to their subject matter.

An open-hearted teacher is called to be fully present and vulnerable. When struggling with this great task, I am inspired by the courage of Bronson Alcott, when he said:

The true teacher defends his pupils against his own personal influence. He inspires self-trust. He guides their eyes from himself to the spirit that quickens him. He will have no disciples.

Ultimately, we can only teach the whole person before us. Yet, after centuries of intellectualizing and specializing, we have cultivated a generation of educators who insist that they are only hired to instruct a student's mind. Some professors even declare on the first day of class that students should leave the rest of their lives out in the hall. This is not only disrespectful and self-defeating, it is impossible.

Imagine that the greatest instance of knowledge or wisdom we can offer is crystalized into a drop of colored tea and imagine each student before us is a glass of clear water. When we chance to place that drop of knowledge into a student's mind, it will beautifully permeate the student's entire being. You can't just isolate the top inch of water, for the smallest drop is absorbed throughout the entire glass. And you can't just teach to a student's mind, for whatever you offer will permeate the entire being sitting before you.

Once a student's being is stirred, the terrain of education shifts to one of dialogue. Only by applying inner to outer can we find our place in the Universe. And only through expression and honest dialogue can we discover what's real and useful.

More broadly, the encouragement of expression is vital to our culture because we now suffer from an epidemic of suppression. One way to heal this rupture is to instill a deep regard for expression in our children. Then, in time, the cultural gulf between inner and outer and the schism between self and other will diminish across our society, so that speaking our minds and hearts before others will not be such a traumatic event to be avoided.

As it is, knowledge is too often imparted with no regard for the whole person receiving it. And once receiving it, there is seldom any space to express and dialogue about what has been received in a way that pertains to the life we are living.

In truth, if what we teach can't be traced to an inner necessity to do so, then its place in our curriculum should be questioned. And the greatest teachers defer being seen as great. They point to the greatness of life that is available to everyone. With a determined kindness, they bring the cup to their student's lip, then show their students how to make a cup for when they find the water for themselves.

*An honest classroom depends on the integrity and compassion of the teacher, who is the one in the room asking the most questions and taking the most risks.*

## Questions to Walk With

- The French philosopher Rabelais said, "A child is a fire to be lit, not a vase to be filled." In your journal, discuss a time when a teacher tried to fill you like a vase and another time when a teacher tried to light you like a fire. What is your relationship with each of these teachers?
- In conversation with a friend or loved one, exchange stories about a teacher along the way who welcomed all of you into their classroom. How did this affect how you see the world?

# Between Fear and Welcome

SOMEHOW, EACH GENERATION is called to enliven their care as a way to ensure that the world will continue. Just as all vegetation depends on the thousands of pollinations that take place each spring, life depends on the thousands of ways we each face our struggle and inhabit our possibility. Rather than fix the world, we are here to inhabit it. And it all begins with the courage to be honest and authentic. For those efforts, no matter how imperfectly engaged, will return us to our basic nature.

As the thirst of a horse will make it drink from the nearest stream, we are each born with a thirst for the river of light wherever it appears. Even though this yearning toward Wholeness is inborn, it takes courage to drink so directly from life. In his seminal book *The Soul's Code,* the Jungian psychologist James Hillman expresses his "acorn theory of the soul" where, as the full grown oak is waiting to evolve from the acorn, our soul's expressive energy is waiting to grow out of the seed of our Spirit that starts to germinate within us the moment we are born.

The very personal way that our heart brings the expressive energy we were born with into the world is our soul's journey. An essential part of our personal spiritual practice, then, is to become intimate with our soul's journey, learning how to listen to it. How can you inhabit your life in such a way that your path can bring your soul into the world?

When we can be present and stay in relationship, our capacity to transform and grow keeps evolving. The reach of our heart's connection is ever-deepening and ever-expanding. In time, we discover that the perennial antidotes to fear and misanthropic thinking are the commitments to be wholehearted and to work with what we're given. In truth, if another world is possible, it is this world enlivened with our care. For restoring our deep, unwavering presence in the world will often give us fresh eyes. And this newly cleansed way of seeing will often right-size the problem at hand and help us to see the one action that will keep the problem from growing.

Consider how millions of years ago, a small feathered creature the size of a crow began to loft itself from tree to tree. It was a weak glider. This was the beginning of flight. Today, the Arctic tern migrates 44,000 miles from Greenland to the Wendell Sea in Antarctica. A few million years ago, small primates began to walk upright when they lost the ability to cling to branches. And thousands of years later, the brain started stitching its neural networks when we began to reach for each other.

All this affirms that, even when we fail, our reach, in time, may reveal a new way of being in the world. When we can no longer cling, we may finally start to fly. Is it any wonder that the locus of care we call the heart keeps evolving? Any wonder that a small child in Australia can run her hand in the water and sense the sun rising over a stream somewhere else in the world where an old woman slouches to think of all the children coming of age around the world?

And so, we could say that faith, beyond any dogma or formal tradition, is our belief in the reach of the connections inherent to all life. We could also say that faith is our covenant with life no matter what befalls us. It is our belief that we are part of something larger than us. It is our commitment to let all that is larger than us be our teacher. What light is for plants and flowers, faith is for human souls. It is that which causes us to grow and that toward which we grow. And though we are always moving between fear and welcome, we are constantly challenged to live together.

Imagine a seed growing underground toward a light it can't yet see. In just this way, love and suffering cause us to break ground and flower. We break ground by following our heart, by being real, by being kind. This stirring, this breaking ground, this flowering is our transformation. When full of faith—full of our belief in life—we reveal the force that joins us. There are many names for this force. Some call it God. Some call it Allah. Some call it the Holy Ghost. Some call it Yahweh. Some call it the Collective Unconscious. Some call it Atman. Some call it Oneness. Some call it the Great Spirit. Some call it Nature. Some just call it life-force. I welcome it by any name. It has saved my life.

> *If another world is possible, it is this*
> *world enlivened with our care.*

## Questions to Walk With

- In your journal, describe the expressive, creative energy you were born with and the various ways it has manifest through you into the world. What way is it wanting to express itself now?
- In conversation with a friend or a loved one, describe your sense of your soul's journey.

# To Admire

THE ANTIDOTE TO pessimism is admiration. It sounds so simple, but the counterpoint to dwelling on what is missing is to affirm what is already here. To live a life of admiration is to name what is uplifting in the world and, through our love and attention, to discern how what matters works, so we can bring it to bear on all that life offers. Through admiration, we address what is missing the way light addresses dark.

The word *admire* came into common usage in the late sixteenth century, from the Latin *admirari*, "to wonder at," "to look at with wonder." Just what does it mean to *look at with wonder*? What does it mean to admire someone or something? How does admiration work? What does it do to us to be admired? What does it do to us to be admiring?

The notion of wonder traces back to the Old English word *wundor*, which meant "marvelous thing, miracle, [or] object of astonishment." When we admire someone or something, we lean into the power of life-force we find there so completely that we are astonished at the existent nature of whatever is before us. For to affirm what is steadfast and foundational, no matter where we find it, enlivens us.

Admiration is a powerful resource because when we admire someone or something, we are, if open, introduced to where those qualities live in us. Then, it is our work to stay in conversation with those qualities, to discern how to water them and nurture them. It is our work to let those qualities of admiration grow from within us out into the world.

I mentioned earlier that the word *respect* means "to look again." And so, by looking at what we admire, again and again, we invoke respect as a way to understand what it is we admire and how we might grow those qualities in similar ways.

When we don't look at what is before us in wonder and don't make the effort to see the seed of what we admire in ourselves, we lose respect for the life around us and within us. Then, we can trip into the traps of scarcity. Unable to see the possibility of what we admire in our own lives, we can become jealous of what we see. Unable to establish our own worth as a spirit in a body in time on Earth, we can become mired in envy, whereby we are so pained to see what we lack in others that we want to deprive them of their gifts. This dark spiral away from our own possibility is insidious.

What, then, does it mean to *look at with wonder*? It means that we receive the life before us as immanently sufficient unto itself. When we look with wonder, we are seeing the inherent Unity of Nature in whatever we look at, be it a butterfly or a wave or the tenderness of a child sleeping. In essence, life-force glows from within each part of the Universe and, if we are open-hearted, each part will mirror our own possibility of being immanently sufficient. While I can't fly like a butterfly, I can turn toward the lightness of being that waits under all my trouble. While I can't exist like a wave, I can turn toward my own resilience which swells, crests, and thins repeatedly no matter what I am called to face. And while I can't regain the innocence of that child sleeping, I can turn toward my remembrance of how rare it is to be alive in any given moment.

So, what does it mean, then, to admire someone or something? It means that we recognize the inherent gifts in what is before us. While I admire the depth of Rainer Maria Rilke, I don't want to be him. I am, rather, encouraged to swim in my own depths. While I admire the honesty of Stanley Kunitz, I don't want to be him. I am, rather, encouraged to uncover my own honesty. While I admire the kaleidoscopic compassion of Pablo Neruda, I don't want to be him. I am, rather, encouraged to expand the color and vision of my own compassion.

And what does it do to us to be admired? The way that light causes everything it touches to open and grow, receiving the attention of admiration causes that piece of life to open and grow further for being seen and affirmed. When you affirm the unwavering ability of a dear friend to listen, you strengthen their gift of listening, empowering them to grow, the way a rose opens after a long day of sunshine.

And what does it do to us to be admiring? We, in turn, grow toward what we admire while strengthening our own versions of those qualities. When I admire horses for how they gallop with all four hooves off the ground, it strengthens my own ability to be wholehearted, even if briefly. When I admire how our dog loves without hesitation, it enlivens my own possibility of holding nothing back. And when I admire how water is both reflective and transparent without losing any of itself, it strengthens my deepest sense of self to be more fully engaged with the world.

So, I invite you to become a student of admiration. What do you look at with wonder? What do you admire specifically in the people, animals, and aspects of nature that thrive around you? What do these specific gifts mirror of your own possibility to live life fully? What steps can you take to become better acquainted with the seeds of these gifts that are dormant within you?

Make a practice of asking for stories of admiration and telling such stories. Tell the people you admire what it is about them that you look at with wonder, and also tell these stories to someone who doesn't yet know these people. So that stories of admiration spread and grow. For to look at life with wonder is the remedy of Spirit arcing between all living things. This leads us to a life where one care uplifts another, joining us across the ages.

## Care Unto Care

In 1689 in Japan, a kind farmer gave the lost poet Basho a horse that knew the way. And in 1910 when Ted Shawn was paralyzed, before he knew he was a dancer, a dear friend left crutches just out of reach and breakfast on the table. And in 1938 in Paris, Django Reinhardt's brother left a guitar at the foot of his hospital bed because he knew the badly burned genius would no longer be able to play the banjo. And when Claude Monet at eighty-two was suffering from double cataracts, he somehow knew to keep painting what he saw, which led him to retrieve his masterful *Water Lilies*. Even leafcutter ants in Costa Rica will carry another ant for miles. These examples are evidence that there is an eternal impulse at the core of all living things that compels us to bridge what is with what can be. And this ounce of care—that skips from living thing to living thing, from generation to generation—keeps life going. This ounce of care connects us all throughout the ages. And so, the care in the farmer's hand giving the reins of his horse to Basho continues in the dancer's friend as he leaves crutches just out of reach and on into Django's brother placing that guitar at the foot of his brother's bed. These acts of care are all parts of one unending gesture that waits in each of us to bring living things together. All of this makes you cry out "Stop!" when we pass a turtle in the middle of the road. And you feel compelled with an urge that rises in you from centuries to get out of the car and place the turtle on the other side of the road.

*When we admire someone or something, we are,*
*if open, introduced to where those qualities live in us.*

## Questions to Walk With

- In your journal, tell a story about someone you admire for what they do for others, and a story about someone you admire for their integrity. Discuss why you admire these people.

- In conversation with someone you admire, ask for the story of how they became who they are. What are their greatest gifts and how did they learn how to use them? What were or are their greatest obstacles? And what were or are their greatest teachers?

# Inside Everything

THE HUMBLING MYSTERY inherent in all attempts at writing is that the words are like the dirt you dig out of a hole. There's so much of it piled all around you as you stand there, sweating from all that digging. Yet all that matters is the opening that is left, which keeps drawing you further in.

And from that depth, I can say that if there is an undertaking at the center of this book, it is to devote yourself to gathering the self-knowledge of how your heart works. In the belief that through this ongoing practice, your heart will become your teacher. In the belief that if we stay connected to our heart, it will guide us to the center of all storms and connect us to the Living Universe. Our job, then, is to stay authentic, open, and vulnerable. These commitments to honest living will make a conduit of the heart, so it can naturally infuse us with the resources of life.

Still, no one can bypass the journey to being authentic. When young, I was so busy pleasing others that I was hiding pieces of myself from the world. Quickly, I was defined by what others needed until if they were on fire, I would throw myself on them like water. If they were inching like a root, I would pack myself around them like soil. If they were bleeding, I would soak up their hurt like a bandage. Sadly, I could only be what was missing. I had no idea who I was or where to go to find out.

I so lost myself in others that I secretly pushed the other way and spent the first half of my life trying to define who I am by how I was different, only to discover that who I really am is defined by what I have in common with all living things. And all along, I was stumbling on a journey of love and truth that kept me smack in the middle of what it means to be alive.

The enduring truth is that while we can always learn from others, no one can teach us how to be human or how to receive each other with compassion. In this, great love and great suffering have always been the teachers. All the spiritual traditions offer various ways and practices to erode our internal resistance to life. Yet, whether we learn from the traditions or not, every person will be given the opportunity to be dropped into the depth of life. We often resist this and fall into an argument with life, which we have to let go of in order to fully experience the miracle of being here.

The challenge for each of us is to enter life beyond our argument with an open heart and to meet trouble and help without preference. For, under all our resistance, the mystery of incarnation is that all the wisdom in the world will not relieve us from the weight of living but only support us in our turn at being here. And though the deepest work is internal and personal, we are not alone.

Arwa Qutbuddin, a young mother from India, has said, "What matters is that we teach our children kindness in a world that is wounded by a lack of it." This is a perennial struggle that each life, each family, each nation, and each generation faces: how to be brave and loving enough to rekindle the kindness we so lack in a world struggling not to give into fear. Now it is our turn. For the future of love depends on the tenderness and honesty of those who can bear witness to the depth of soul rising through their pain. This is the deep remedy we need.

If Hell is dying repeatedly without ever feeling whole, then Heaven is the removal of any false or limited way of thinking or feeling that keeps us from being completely alive. And the heart is the unseeable bridge that offers us this pilgrimage. If blessed, our heart-work leads us from Hell to Heaven in some small way every day. If I could take you there, I would. But I am still making my way myself.

Having dug my way completely out of words, again, I offer you this small poem of mine, with which I wish you a lifetime of listening to the guidance of your heart:

### Inside Everything

Keep trying to hide and in time
you become a wall.

Keep trying to love and in time
you become love.

Our journey on Earth is to stop
hiding, so we can become love.

Everything else is a seduction
and a distraction.

Courage is staying true.

*If Hell is dying repeatedly without ever feeling whole, then Heaven is the removal of any false or limited way of thinking or feeling that keeps us from being completely alive.*

## Questions to Walk With

- In your journal, describe your argument with life and where you are in your journey with it.
- In conversation with a friend or loved one, have each of you discuss your own struggle between trying to hide and trying to love.

# *The Heart Is Still Our Teacher*

———

The space within the heart is as great as the vast universe. The heavens and the earth are there, and the sun and the moon and the stars. Fire and lightning and winds are there, and all that now is and all that is not.

—Swami Prabhavananda

To live with a fidelity to the light that comes from within us and to the light that grows between us—what else is there? No other devotion will free us or sustain us in such an enduring way.

—MN

THIS FINAL SECTION explores the resources that will help us:

- inhabit the forces that ground us more than the forces that incite us,
- and surrender to the peaceful center we are worn to that waits in the center of all storms.

Life never stops coming and when all else fails, the heart is still our teacher. Once we put down our masks, all our efforts go toward uncovering a greater sense of living. This requires a daily vigilance in opening the small room of our mind by devoting ourselves to the blessing of the ordinary. In this way, we have a chance to keep returning to our largest home of all—*Life*. In this way, we have a chance to love each other through our suffering. In this way, we have a glorious chance to rediscover the ground of truth that waits inside everything. The chapters in this final section try to usher you back into the world with the hope that all we have explored in these pages will fill you with the strength to survive whatever storms arise. And through the courage to love everything, may we all be blessed with the gift of more life.

# Toward a Greater Sense of Living

I came across *The Secret Oral Teaching in Tibetan Buddhist Sects.* There, this compelling distinction is made:

> The most striking of the Tibetan Buddhist doctrines in the Secret Teachings concerns *the going beyond.* This doctrine is based on the concept of *Prajna Paramita.* The Tibetans have given the term *Prajna Paramita* a very different meaning from that attributed to it by Indian authors and their Western translators. According to the latter, *Prajna Paramita* means *excellent wisdom, the best, the highest wisdom,* whereas the Tibetans translate this concept as *going beyond wisdom.*

How we understand this makes a huge difference in how we live our lives. For "excellent wisdom, the best, the highest wisdom" implies a state of knowing that we aspire to arrive at or attain. This is more in keeping with a Greek sense of perfection. But a wisdom we "go beyond" implies that wisdom itself is a threshold that we are called to cross into a yet deeper experience of living. It implies that inhabiting wisdom leads to a more enlivening experience, which exists beyond the doorways that knowledge opens.

Whether we attain something or experience it changes everything. Consider the Buddhist virtues that Tibetans hold as sacred.

Some of these virtues include: kindness, patience, energy or effort, meditation or concentration of mind, and transcendent wisdom. These timeless practices are much more compelling as learnings to journey through than as aspects of character we have to live up to.

When we view these virtues as a moral checklist, we work to arrive at a summit of character that is impossible to maintain. But when we can inhabit these virtues, they become, more deeply, portals or thresholds through which we enter a more heartened experience of Oneness, Harmony, or Unity.

This presents two very different approaches to education: whether we struggle to arrive or move through. The effort toward perfection evokes a persistent sense of learning that aspires to arrive at some ideal of behavior, while the effort to go beyond evokes a transformative sense of learning that calls for us to live more complete lives by moving through ever-deepening thresholds.

The common definition of virtue, as behavior showing high moral standards, is admirable and essential unto itself. Yet without the vow to keep growing more deeply, more authentically, and more completely, the common notion of virtue can become a ladder we can never quite climb by which we stubbornly judge ourselves and others for always falling short.

But if we give a larger context to our aspirations, our virtue takes on more enduring meaning. As I mentioned earlier, the Roman philosopher Plotinus defined virtue as "our tendency toward Unity." Add to this the fact that the word *integrity* comes from the Latin meaning "to make whole." Within this larger context, virtue is more about an embodied congruence with life's forces than a moral rectitude that stems from upholding agreed-upon behavior.

This all came up again, recently, when I fell into a sweeping discussion with two dear friends, George and Don. All three of us are teachers. I convene circles around living an authentic life, while George teaches Tai Chi, and Don teaches watercolor painting. We were together on a Saturday afternoon in early February when Don suddenly asked, "What does composition mean to you?"

We quickly agreed that a strong sense of composition, in any art or act of building or repair, centers on the parts all serving to create a more liberating whole. The question stayed with me and later in the day, the two conversations—the one about virtue and the one about composition—began to stir within me.

As an individual soul trying to make good use of my heart and as a lifelong teacher retrieving insight after insight, all my work centers on the transformative vow to learn by going through and beyond. And so, whether I'm designing a weekend retreat or a yearlong journey or framing the chapter that begins a book, composition for me begins with the commitment to identify archetypal portals or thresholds of human depth and life-giving connection, through which we might enter the underlying nature and Unity of Life. Then, I enter these portals myself, retrieving questions of introspection and dialogue that can help each of us personalize and integrate the aspects of Oneness we might discover in our daily lives.

Yet how do we discover what *going beyond* means in a daily way? I have found that working with the thresholds of presence, meaning, and relationship is a helpful way to practice virtue and integrity. And since the word *educate* means "to draw out, to call forth what is already present," perhaps our journey through the days is one of self-education: of calling forth through experience that which is already present within us—until, through presence, meaning, and relationship, we find that the world is within us and our essence is in the world.

Perhaps this is how St. Francis could be in conversation with birds and walk with wolves, how Claude Monet could paint light as it conversed with water against the stones at Étretat, and how Beethoven in his irrevocable silence could reveal the immense tide of harmonies that he later called the *Ninth Symphony*.

I keep returning to how the great sociologist Ivan Illich defined Spiritual Hospitality—as the effort to help another cross a threshold. And I happily confess that all my writing and teaching have been and continue to be efforts in Spiritual Hospitality.

If we are to inhabit the soul's work on Earth, the deepest and most revealing form of education is not to amass knowledge but to keep deepening our ability to know. And the most enduring and inwardly practical form of education is to keep helping each other cross threshold after threshold.

> *Wisdom itself is a threshold that we are called*
> *to cross into a yet deeper experience of living.*

## Questions to Walk With

- In your journal, describe an experience you moved through that helped you make better use of your gifts. What enlarged sense of knowing was awakened in you and how did that new knowing enable you to inhabit your gifts more fully?

# The Other Wing

BEFORE ANYONE WAS around to see, a very large bird, gliding above a fast-moving river, saw something small and dark scurrying below. The bird tipped its wing and dove, only to find the thing scurrying was its own shadow. And with the tip of its other wing, it rose again into the sky. This fleeting, unnoticed moment holds the crossroads of the human journey. For trying to eat our shadow without realizing it is at the heart of all addiction. While tipping the other wing is at the heart of all transformation.

What does "tipping the other wing" mean? It speaks to the hard-earned wisdom of seeing things as they are and then accepting that truth in time to save ourselves. It means not compounding our misperception by distorting what is true. It means we have to remember that the second half of stumbling is admitting when we are wrong. It means not insisting on a map that has proved false.

Tipping the other wing means giving up life positions such as victim, judge, and rescuer. It means washing our eyes with truth and rinsing our heart with love. Every day, one of us sights some dark thing scurrying below and we dive, thinking it will feed the pain we show no one. And often, the most crippling moment that can befall us is to catch the dark shadow we chase. For eating our own shadow makes us prisoners of the chase. But once we stop chasing, we can be thankful for all of it. The way a pilgrim who breaks his leg at the top of a mountain is thankful for the view.

And what does eating our own shadow mean? This speaks to when we are trapped in our own tangle of wounds and confusion, unable to access a viewpoint beyond our own pain and fear. When trapped this way, we are like the Egyptian serpent Uroboros, who is forever eating his own tail. Yet, when washed over by great love or great suffering, we can be broken of this painful cycle.

Coming in and out of awareness like this is very humbling and inescapably part of being human. And so, in the tangle of our days, much of our inner health depends on the courage to return to being aware when we are stymied by mental and emotional confusions that mislead us: as when a lack of worth makes me interpret every comment as a slight, or when a recurring fear makes me see every approaching sign of life as a threat, or when a wound of love gone wrong makes me mistrust all acts of kindness. When chasing these shadows, we can be misled for months or even years, under the influence of a dream, a wound, or an expectation that has eluded or hurt us. If we remain unaware, these confusions are never corrected, and the weight and press of unprocessed thought and emotion can dominate our personality and even become a way of life. For example, I can become a skeptical person who distrusts life or someone in constant need of attention and approval.

But the power of honest self-awareness is always available to us and partaking in it can free us from the trance of moods that overcome us. If I am feeling less than and insufficient and I remain unaware of the inner pain this keeps causing me, I will relentlessly keep seeking approval and affirmation from everyone around me until I suffocate the possibility of true relationship and become even more isolated. Yet through honest self-awareness, I can accept this sense of insufficiency and address the lack within me directly. This is the tip of the other wing that always leads to healing.

It seems that, all too often, the trance of our moods has us relive the pains of a troubled heart, while authentic growth is the gradual expansion of a self-awareness that restores our unmitigated sense of being alive. So when chasing a speck of worth or finding myself trapped in a cycle of codependence, I can recognize what is going on and say to myself, "Oh, I know what this is. I've been here before." Then, we can tip the other wing and course-correct.

In truth, I don't think we can ever rid ourselves completely from the weight and press of unprocessed thought and emotion. But it is the work of self-awareness, honest and thorough, that minimizes the time we spend being thrown under by these difficult trances of mood. I've come to understand that being awake means that, instead of remaining hidden and crippled by what takes hold of us, we recognize what is happening ever more swiftly. Then, like a dancer who stumbles and goes on, the trance of mood is only a misstep that we incorporate into the dance of our lives. We leap, fall, incorporate the misstep, and dance on!

Ultimately, the practice of releasing ourselves from illusion is the inner give and take by which we recognize the trance we are under—whatever that might be—and that recognition allows us to restore our direct experience of unfiltered life. This is a never-ending process. And so, enlightenment is not a state we arrive at but a devotion to our cyclical participation in the ebb and flow of light within us and around us that makes life, for long moments, clear and bearable. Enlightenment is the continual unfolding of awareness that comes and goes like sunrise and sunset over the landscape of our life.

> *The second half of stumbling is*
> *admitting when we are wrong.*

## Questions to Walk With

- In your journal, describe a trance of mood that has gripped you and misled you. It might be a way of thinking or feeling imposed upon you by a parent or a partner. It might be a sense of being a victim or judge or rescuer. It might be an image of your self-worth or an unlived dream that haunts you. Describe the tip of wing that entraps you there, how you are drawn under the influence of this mood. Then, describe the tip of wing that releases you, how you are lifted from the influence of this mood and brought back into your direct experience of being alive.

- In conversation with a friend or loved one, discuss your history of working with a mental or emotional state that plagues you. How has the pattern of this state or mood changed over time? How has your self-awareness of this state or mood and your release from it changed over time?

# Returning to the Moment

I want to learn more and more to see as beautiful what is necessary ... then I shall be one of those who makes things beautiful.

—Friedrich Nietzsche

This offering from Nietzsche during the latter part of his life might be the anthem of our day. For we are being challenged to make what is necessary beautiful. For instance, during the pandemic, we were asked to wash our hands many times a day. While doing so, it occurred to me that we can also wash our minds and hearts daily. So we can return to what matters when fear and worry entangle us. So we can find the foundational ground of being below all the complications of the surface world. So we can return to the moment we are in over the dream or dread of the future and the hardened stories of our past.

In personalizing the work of washing our mind and heart, we are asked to make good use of stillness, mindfulness, and wholeheartedness, as ways to refresh our sense of just being born—so we can see and feel things anew. The efforts to listen, care, and give also scour our lens and bring us back to what matters. This is what it means to return to the moment: that we remove all that grows in the way so we can know life directly one more time. This freshness of being and perception doesn't remove all our problems but it gives us access to a reservoir of being that lives beneath our troubles.

Yet being in the moment does not mean that we are meant to dwell in our personal circumstances alone. This is just the beginning of our awareness. For being in the moment is an apprenticeship for being in the One Ongoing Eternal Moment that is happening everywhere at all times. By being fully present to what's before me, with nothing in the way, I cross a threshold of presence that lets me receive the many instances of life happening everywhere at the same time.

It's how I can suddenly be aware of the birth of a child halfway around the world while I am suffering. If I only *think* of this, I might not be able to make sense of the myriad forms of experience or trace their common source of life. But when inhabiting what is before me, I can enter the One Ongoing Eternal Moment through the moment I am in. Then, I can *feel* the life-force of that child being born flow toward my suffering, the way water fills every hole.

Our inner well-being depends on our continual awareness that life is not just what is happening to us. As one cell gives us access to the nature of all cells, one moment entered completely gives us access to life everywhere. And washing our minds and hearts of all that sticks to them allows us to inhabit the restorative connection between all things.

Essentially, each moment is a practice ground for us to come alive by removing whatever grows in the way. So, think of each moment as a threshold or portal to the rest of life. Think of being completely where you are as the necessary initiation we each must make if we are to feel the flow of life between us and others, between us and every living creature, between us and the changing landscapes that make up this Earth, between us and the elements that bring life into being, and between us and the invisible current of life that sustains us all.

*Being in the moment is an apprenticeship for*
*being in the One Ongoing Eternal Moment that*
*is happening everywhere at all times.*

## Questions to Walk With

- As a meditation, enter the moment you are in completely. First, feel everything near you from the dust on the table to the tree branch outside your window. Then, feel the details of your inwardness at this moment: the places you are calm, the places you are agitated, the places you are tender. Now, in your journal, describe the many instances of life happening in concentric rings at the same time as the moment you are in: starting with next door, then on the next street, then in the next county, state, across the country, and in several places around the world. Receive and imagine a particular scene of life in each instance. Finally, describe how all these instances of life happening at once affect each other and you.
- In conversation with a friend or loved one, discuss one daily practice you can enlist to wash your mind and heart of their assumptions and conclusions.

# The Blessing of the Ordinary

IN A MOMENT of exhaustion, my mind was too tired to keep weaving its web and my heart too tired to keep the world at bay. In that sudden stillness, I realized that, as a patch of water when still will reveal the bottom of a lake, the blessing of the ordinary is that any moment met with stillness will reveal the whole of life that resides under everything.

This is the power of presence. When fully present, we can see through to the center of all storms. Through meditation, we can breathe our way back into presence. Through love, we are softened back into presence. And through suffering, we are broken back into presence. However we get there, dropping below the surface of things returns us to the heart of all being, which sustains the kinship between all things. When fully present, however briefly, we drink from the Unities and are renewed. In deep ways, poetry, music, and art in all their forms are life-sustaining because they lead us to these moments. It is our ongoing practice to enter them and drink again from life.

In truth, my life as a poet has led me to seek out these moments as teachers. All my writing has been no more than one long conversation with these moments, trying to map their lessons. And beyond any insights I may have stumbled on, it is drinking from the Unities underneath these moments that has kept me vital and awake.

Honest and tender relationships also lead us to these moments. The word *interview* comes from the French *entrevue,* which means "the view between." And so, true dialogue is not one person questioning another, but both using their love and honesty to still the turbulence of their days in order to see through to the bottom of things, where we can drink of life together. In the most vulnerable of these moments, we lift the cup of life to each other's lips.

We often trip into these see-through moments when in nature. We might be stopped by the spray of light through a canopy of trees as it wavers on and off the path we didn't know was there. Or when quietly stunned by a doe drinking from a stream. Or when placing our palm on the trunk of a thousand-year-old redwood. We might drop below our worry when watching the surf creep closer to our feet, a wave at a time. Or when glimpsing the horizon through a shelf of clouds after a long and winding hike up an unmarked trail.

Just yesterday, I was having coffee on our deck. And watching our dog roll on her back in the grass, the sun on her belly, I saw through and felt the glow of Oneness connecting all things. It brought me to a spot of inexplicable peace.

These see-through moments reveal the well of being that holds everything together. Light often leads us to them. A few years ago, in New York City, I was on my way to meet my editor, running late, when the light through the awning of a bodega rippled across the neck of a pigeon pecking at crumbs. I was stopped. For something in the light was saying, "Wherever you are rushing, what you are looking for is here, in the neck of the lighted pigeon. Where else would you rather be?"

When these moments open, I have learned to just be more present. Rather than trying to figure out what is happening, I try to still my mind until all things go clear, so I can see through to the place where everything touches everything else. In these present, still moments, I am briefly enlightened—that is, I am lighted within. And this infusion of kinship changes everything.

Painters have always been drawn to paint such moments. The Impressionists, in particular, were compelled to bring into view what the light was pointing to. Consistently, there is an incandescence in these legendary canvases that lets us see through. And all true poems land there. In fact, all true expressions, written down or not, open that see-through spot. When turning inward, we are blessed to discover that each soul, when holding nothing back, is such a see-through moment. To be this present, we need a sustained courage to be who we are everywhere and to love everything in the way. For such inner courage leads us to the blessing of the ordinary.

So, when we come upon each other, all agitated by the wind of trouble, wait for one of us to go clear, like that patch of water that briefly reveals the bottom of a lake. Listen to me and, in time, I will go transparent. Then, because of the care of your listening, I will be able to see through into the heart of your being, too. Then, together, as lovers and friends have done for centuries, we will touch into the heart of all being and feel something sacred joining us. Then, for the rest of our lives, we will know that spot of unnamable truth as a holiness we can return to, alone and together. Any moment will open and bring us there. Even this moment now.

*Any moment met with stillness will reveal the*
*whole of life that resides under everything.*

## Questions to Walk With

- For your last journal question, describe a moment you came upon that you were able to enter when still enough. What opened for you in this moment? How did entering this moment affect you? How would you describe what this moment opened you to?
- For your last conversation question, listen to each other until the view between you goes clear like that patch of water in a lake. Then, look through to the bottom of things together. Describe what you see.

# The Love of Everything

So here we are, at the end of another long conversation, the trail of which is this book. As always, on this quiet precipice between feeling and speaking, I worry that I've said too much and wonder if it's not enough. In truth, all we've unearthed and looked at, all we've listened to and unraveled, has merely mirrored the spark we carry called life.

The only thing left to say is that, after more than seventy years, I confess that, even when struggling, even when lost, I have never stopped loving—everything. And this has enabled me to inhabit life authentically. In the beginning, there were goals I was taught to work toward and these longings for worth were honed in time into personal ambitions, which all fell away. For staying true to the love of everything as our teacher has turned out to be the most enduring ambition of all.

This love has made me get up when I have fallen, and has given me the strength to enter the breaks in my heart where I have retrieved my gifts. And so, I have very little to offer beyond the affirmation that unending love without preference will lead us to drink from the Mystery without leaving the world. Unending love without intent will fill every contour of existence the way light fills every hole. So, there is very little to teach. Just that love awakens everything. And care erases the walls we keep building between us.

# GRATITUDES

I am grateful to my teachers, including my father, Morris Nepo, the Renaissance scholar Hugh McClean, the Jungian teacher Helen Luke, my woodblock teacher Mary Brodbeck, and my contemporaries, the poets Marge Piercy, Phil Levine, and Naomi Shihab Nye. As well, a deep bow to the Chinese poet of the Tang dynasty Tu Fu, the great Chilean poet Pablo Neruda, the great Austrian poet Rainer Maria Rilke, the irrepressible Walt Whitman, and the steadfast William Carlos Williams.

I'm also grateful to my agent, Eve Atterman, for her deep care and vitality, and to James Munro and Fiona Baird and the WME team for their commitment through the years. And to Brooke Warner, my trusted first reader for many years, for her wisdom and care. And to my publisher-editor, Joel Fotinos, who serves as a lighthouse for literature. And to my publicist, Eileen Duhne, for bridging me to the world. And to my former agent, Jennifer Rudolph Walsh, for welcoming me so heartily years ago.

Gratitude to my dear friends, each a teacher in how they live. Especially George, Don, Paul, Skip, TC, David, Parker, Kurt, Pam, Patti, Karen, Paula, Ellen, Dave, Jill, Jacquelyn, Linda, Michelle, Rich, Carolyn, Henk, Elesa, Penny, Sally, and Joel. And to Jamie Lee Curtis for the strength of her kindness. And to Oprah Winfrey for believing that life is the greatest teacher.

And to Paul Bowler for all he's taught me about caring for others. And to Robert Mason for teaching me how to face the wind and sing. And to my dear wife, Susan, a great teacher of all things heart.

—MN

# NOTES

Epigraphs and poems without attribution are by the author.

**p. xiii, epigraph:** "**Remember . . .**": Abraham Heschel, in an interview taped for NBC ten days before his death, from *I Asked for Wonder: A Spiritual Anthology*, selections from Abraham Heschel, edited by Samuel H. Dresner. Pearl River, NY: Crossroads Books, 1999, p. viii.

## PART 1: WHERE WE ARE

### MAPPING THE FAULT LINES

#### The Old World Is Gone

**p. 5: "the word *sabbath* . . .":** For an in-depth exploration of the sabbath, see the modern classic *Sabbath* by Wayne Muller, New York: Random House, 2000.

**p. 7: "Adrift":** First appeared in my book *Inside the Miracle: Enduring Suffering, Approaching Wholeness*. Louisville, CO: Sounds True, 2015, p. 217.

#### Our Refracted Society

**p. 10: "Karl Marx . . .":** My first exploration of our history of alienation appeared in the chapter "Blind Travelers" in my book *More Together Than Alone*. New York: Atria Books, 2018, p. 173.

**p. 10: "As early as 1844 . . . basic human nature":** Alienation is a theme that runs throughout the work of Karl Marx (1818–1883), beginning with his *Economic and Philosophical Manuscripts* of 1844.

**p. 11: "These estrangements . . .":** Many sociologists of the late nineteenth and early twentieth centuries were concerned about the alienating effects of modernization pointed to by Marx. German sociologists Georg Simmel (1858–1918) and Ferdinand Tönnies (1855–1936) wrote seminal works on individualization and urbanization. Simmel's *Philosophy of Money (Philosophie des Geldes)* explores how relationships become more and more diluted through money, while Tönnies's *Community and Society (Gemeinschaft und Gesellschaft)* describes the loss of primary relationships such as family bonds in favor of goal-oriented relationships.

**p. 13: "reality shows . . .":** My first exploration of reality TV culture appeared in the chapter "Living in Fear and Scarcity" in my book *More Together Than Alone*. New York: Atria Books, 2018, p. 66.

**p. 18: "*World Report on Violence and Health . . .*":** Geneva: World Health Organization, 2002, p. 8. The following four paragraphs originally appeared in the chapter "Our Global Body" in my book *More Together Than Alone*. New York: Atria Books, 2018, p. 254. Updated statistics regarding violence are from "Homicides" by Max Roser and Hannah Ritchie, *World Data*, December 2019, and "One person dies every forty seconds from suicide" by Katie Hunt, *CNN*, Sept 9, 2019.

**p. 20: "On May 25, 2020, George Floyd . . .":** Details in this first paragraph are from Wikipedia, https://en.wikipedia.org/wiki/George_Floyd.

**p. 18: "In 2019 . . . convicted of murder":** Cited on *The ReidOut* with Joy Reid on MSNBC, September 23, 2020.

## The Nature of Storms

**p. 25: "It is only during a storm . . .":** Matshona Dhliwayo is a Canada-based philosopher who was born in Zimbabwe. His many books include *Lalibela's Wise Man.*

**p. 26: "a poem of mine . . .":** "Fighting the Instrument" in my book of poems *The Way Under the Way: The Place of True Meeting*. Louisville, CO: Sounds True Publishing, 2016, p. 14.

**p. 25: "the nature and life of storms . . .":** Details are drawn from an exceptional article on Wikipedia, https://en.wikipedia.org/wiki/Storm.

**p. 28: "common types of storms . . .":** Two of the deadliest storms in history were the Great Galveston Hurricane (1900) which killed close to twelve thousand people, and the 1769 lightning strike of the Church of the Nazaire in Brescia, Italy. The lightning ignited 207,000 pounds of gunpowder. The explosion destroyed a sixth of the city and killed three thousand residents.

**p. 32: "In Medieval Europe . . .":** The notion of Tempestarii is cited by J Skookum, https://www.reddit.com/r/mythology/comments/95xnlp/legendary_storms/.

### The Purpose of Goodness

**p. 35: "Reading Neil deGrasse Tyson . . .":** Details are from *Astrophysics for People in a Hurry.* New York: Norton, 2017, pp. 25–26, 30.

**p. 36: "Cody Howard . . .":** "Marriott Criticized After Ship Leaves Tourists Behind in Caribbean Because They Weren't Guests of the Hotel," Stephanie Petit, *People* magazine, September 13, 2017, http://people.com/human-interest/marriott-ship-leaves-tourists-behind-in-caribbean-because-they-werent-hotel-guests/.

**p. 37: "By this point . . .":** Details about the flight and the radar image are from a paywalled article in the *Miami Herald,* September 6, 2017, http://www.miamiherald.com/news/nation-world/world/article171577632.html.

**p. 38: "They came first . . .":** by Martin Niemöller, in the New England Holocaust Memorial in Boston. This story and the poem are originally cited in my book *More Together Than Alone.* New York: Atria Books, 2018, p. 82.

## PART 2: FINDING THE STRENGTH

**p. 41, epigraph: "We gauge culture . . .":** Abraham Heschel, from *The Earth Is the Lord's: The Inner World of the Jew in Eastern Europe.* NY: Jewish Lights, 1995, pp. 7–10.

**p. 41, epigraph: "You cannot hope . . .":** Marie Curie, from the journal *The Sun,* Issue 532, April 2020, p. 48.

### EVERY PATH HOLDS A QUESTION

#### One Candle Lighting Many

**p. 45: "Thousands of candles . . .":** Attributed to Buddha, a paraphrase of Section 10 of the "Sutra of 42 Sections" in the Japanese text *The Teaching of Buddha.*

**p. 46: "I am going to give up . . .":** From "Marie Curie's Contributions to Radiology During World War I" by A. R. Coppes-Zantinga and M. J. Coppes in *Medical Pediatric Oncology,* Issue 31, 1998, pp. 541–543.

### To Grow What We Know

**p. 50: "See No Stranger":** In *See No Stranger*, the many-gifted Valarie Kaur has birthed a book of utmost resilience, invoking ancient truths as remedies to our tense and polarized modern world, if we can inhabit our greatest gift—love. Her fiercely loving voice is wise beyond her years.

**p. 50: "orientation to wonder . . .":** Valarie Kaur, from *See No Stranger*. New York: One World Books, 2020, p. 10.

### You Can't Fly with One Wing

**p. 53: "Down in their hearts . . .":** Elbert Hubbard, from *The Sun*, Issue 534, June 2020, p. 48.

**p. 53: "Catherine of Siena":** The story of Catherine of Siena (1347–1380) is from *Varieties of Mystical Experience*, edited by Elmer O'Brien. New York: New American Library, 1965, p. 149.

**p. 55: "If you don't know . . .":** William Stafford, from "A Ritual to Read to Each Other" in *The Way It Is: New & Selected Poems*. St. Paul, MN: Graywolf Press, 1998, p. 75.

**p. 55: "Midway this way of life . . .":** Translation by Dorothy Sayers, cited in Helen Luke's *Dark Wood to White Rose: The Journey and Transformation in Dante's Divine Comedy*. New York: Morning Light Press, 1993, p. 4. Helen's inquiry into Dante's epic is one of the most transforming books I've ever read.

### Notes on the True Self

**p. 59: "Notes on the True Self":** I was drawn to gather my thoughts on this topic after a compelling conversation about the True Self with Ashton Gustafson, for his podcast, *Good, True, and Beautiful*, https://ashtongustafson.com/ltmppodcast. Ashton is an old soul who looks deeply into all the ancient corners, bringing what he finds to bear on our modern life.

**p. 60: "We all experience this mysterious process . . .":** The next four paragraphs originally appear in the introduction, "Stewards of Light," to my book *The Long Walk Through Time*.

**p. 63: "Praying I Will Find":** From my book of poems *The Half-Life of Angels*.

**p. 64: "The Moment of Poetry":** From my book of poems *The Way Under the Way: The Place of True Meeting*. Louisville, CO: Sounds True Publishing, 2016, p. 290.

## To Be Radical

**p. 70: "Standing eye to eye with being . . .":** Abraham Heschel, from *Man Is Not Alone*. NY: Farrar, Straus & Giroux, 1951, p. 11.

**p. 71: "Considering that . . .":** W. B. Yeats, from "A Prayer for My Daughter" in *The Poems of W.B. Yeats,* edited by Richard J. Finneran. NY: Macmillan, 1983, p. 188.

**p. 72: "John Paul Lederach . . .":** I am grateful for my many conversations with John Paul. Please see *The Moral Imagination* and *The Journey Toward Reconciliation,* both by John Paul Lederach.

**p. 73: "time more as a pond . . .":** From Professor Dave Edwards, a Cherokee descendant, in the Eiteljorg Native American Museum, Indianapolis, Indiana.

**p. 74: "The Aramaic word for children, *dawnawhie* . . .":** From *Prayer of the Cosmos: Meditations on the Aramaic Words of Jesus,* translated by Neil Douglas-Klotz. CA: HarperSanFrancisco, 1990, p. 66.

## FROM BROKENNESS TO TENDERNESS

**p. 77, epigraph: "Whatever makes living precious . . .":** T'ao Ch'ien, from "Drinking Wine" in *The Selected Poems of Tao Ch'ien,* translated by David Hinton. Port Townsend, WA: Copper Canyon Press, 1993, p. 51.

## The Suffering in Not Suffering

**p. 89: "Maybe the ancient Cynics . . .":** Robert Mason, from his book in manuscript, *Field Guide,* p. 27 Permission of the author.

## A Broken Hallelujah

**p. 97: "it was sung by fifteen hundred souls . . .":** Here are links to the Rufus Wainwright version of "Hallelujah" sung with fifteen hundred souls in Toronto, Canada, on June 11, 2016, as well as to Leonard Cohen's acceptance speech on October 11, 2011, for the Spanish Prince of Asturias Award, and finally, to a live excerpt of Leonard Cohen singing "Hallelujah" himself in mid-life:

*Choir! Choir! Choir! Epic! Nights: Rufus Wainwright + 1500 Singers sing HALLELUJAH!*: https://www.youtube.com/watch?time_continue=17&v=AGRfJ6-qkr4&feature=emb_logo.

*Leonard Cohen's Prince of Asturias Speech* (video and transcript): https://americanrhetoric.com/speeches/leonardcohenhowigotmysong.htm.

*Leonard Cohen Hallelujah* (live excerpt): https://www.youtube.com/watch?time_continue=13&v=kzWeN-bVDUc&feature=emb_title.

**p. 93: "'Hallelujah' is a love song . . .":** from "Leonard Cohen's Holy and Broken Hallelujah" by Alisa Ungar-Sargon, from the journal *Image,* September 19, 2018, https://imagejournal.org/2018/09/19/leonard-cohens-holy-and-broken-hallelujah/.

### Heartwork

**p. 108, epigraph: "Don't be ashamed . . ."** Tomas Tranströmer, from *The Sun,* Issue 517, January 2019, p. 48.

### A THOUSAND STITCHES TILL DAWN

**p. 111, epigraph: "Until we extend . . .":** Albert Schweitzer, from *The Sun,* Issue 529, January 2020, p. 48.

### The Sovereignty of the Seer

**p. 118: "The primary connection . . .":** Martin Buber, *I and Thou.* New York: Scribner Classics, 2000.

**p. 119: "To find the central clue . . .":** Confucius, *The Analects.* New York: Penguin Classics, 1998.

**p. 119: "As for the rest of life . . .":** Friedrich Nietzsche, *Beyond Good and Evil.* New York: Vintage Books, 1989.

**p. 120: "The compulsion to know everything . . ."** E. E. Schattschneider, *In Search of a Government.* New York: Holt, Rinehart, and Winston, 1969.

### The Maturing of Compassion

**p. 125: "Pain that is not felt . . .":** Michael Mejia is a student of mine who lives in Southern California. I've watched Michael grow so authentically into who he is over the past ten years. He has the voice of a young, contemporary Rumi. His honesty and deep presence affirm how our humanness and spirit are knit together. Please see his video "The Humanizing (a story of coming out)," https://www.youtube.com/watch?v=cE-YYX3d5fw&feature=youtu.be.

**p. 125: "There is no unconnected misery"**: Percy Bysshe Shelley (1792–1822), from "Queen Mab" cited in Adrienne Rich's *Poetry & Commitment.* New York: Norton & Co., 2007, p. 7.

**p. 126: "Compassion means . . ."**: Henri Nouwen, from *The Sun,* Issue 498, June 2017, p. 48.

**p. 126: "The purpose of education . . ."**: From *The Journey from Knowing about Community to Knowing Community,* Sally Z. Hare, March 2005, p. 30.

## Inner Triage

**p. 130: "The first evidence . . ."**: Aurelia Clunie, from "Surgery . . . A Violent Profession," Hartford Stage, https://www.hartfordstage.org/stagenotes/ether-dome/history-of-surgery.

## The Paradox of Limitation

**p. 133: "The highest reward . . ."**: John Ruskin (1819–1900), the art critic and watercolorist.

## RESTORING OUR KINSHIPS

**p. 145, epigraph: "Relationship is . . ."**: From *The Religion of Man,* Rabindranath Tagore. Eastford, CT: Martino Fine Books, 2013.

## Doing for Others, Seeing for Ourselves

**p. 148: "The arts are the wilderness areas . . ."**: Claude Lévi-Strauss, cited in *Practice of the Wild,* Gary Snyder. Berkeley, CA: Counterpoint, 1990, p. ix.

**p. 149: "The mystery is . . ."**: From "Tell Me You Have Come" in my book *The Way Under the Way: The Place of True Meeting.* Louisville, CO: Sounds True Publishing, 2016, p. 89.

## Our Need to Learn

**p. 153: "Those who wake . . ."**: From my poem "Unearthed Again" which originally appears in my book of poetry *The Way Under the Way: The Place of True Meeting.* Louisville, CO: Sounds True Publishing, 2016, p. 17.

**p. 154: "embarazar"**: The most common definition of *embarazar* is "to become pregnant."

## Below All Names

**p. 158: "Below All Names":** I first explored this notion in the chapter "The One True World" in my book *The Endless Practice*. New York: Atria Books, 2014, p. 286.

**p. 158: "I was interviewed by Ashton Gustafson":** The interview we did together is recorded in Ashton's podcast called "Good, True, and Beautiful." This episode (#437, Sept 6, 2019) can be heard at https://www.podomatic.com/podcasts/ashtongustafson/episodes/2019–09–06T07_01_48–07_00.

**p. 159: "see a world in a grain of sand":** William Blake, from "Auguries of Innocence" in *William Blake: The Complete Illuminated Books,* edited by David Bindman. London: Thames & Hudson, 2001.

## Straying and Returning

**p. 165: "Judgment and comparison . . .":** Aldous Huxley, from "Preface," in *The First and Last Freedom,* Krishnamurti. San Francisco: HarperSanFrancisco, 1954, p. 17.

**p. 165: "I see that all . . .":** William Cowper, from "I was a Stricken Deer," in *The Soul Is Here for Its Own Joy,* edited by Robert Bly. New York: Ecco Press, 1995, p. 67.

**p. 166: "the medieval doctor Sydenham . . .":** A. Zuger, SH Miles. "Physicians, AIDS, and Occupational Risk: Historic Traditions and Ethical Obligations," *JAMA* 258, 1987, 1924–8.

**p. 170: "Heaven and Earth":** eden ahbez (1908–1995), from his song "The Wanderer" in his album *Eden's Island,* Del-Fi Records, 1960.

## Our Kinship During Adversity

**p. 174: "Towboats along the Yotsugi-dōri Canal . . .":** From *Hiroshige: One Hundred Famous Views of Edo.* New York: George Braziller, 1986, plate 33. Print shown from the Brooklyn Museum of Art.

**p. 174: "That is why . . .":** From "Summary," in *Fully Empowered,* Pablo Neruda, translated by Alastair Reid. New York: Farrar, Straus & Giroux, 1975, p. 121.

## The Restorative Nature of Belief

**p. 178: "In Buddhism, saddha . . .":** I am indebted to the great Buddhist teacher Tara Brach for unpacking the deeper meaning of this.

## THE RUSH OF LIFE

**p. 181, epigraph:** "In our era . . .": from *Markings,* Dag Hammarskjöld. New York: Vintage, 2006, p. xxi.

### The Perennial Choices

**p. 186:** "**Generosity may be more valuable . . .**": Llewellyn Vaughan-Lee, from *A Handbook for Survivalists: Caring for the Earth.* Pt Reyes, CA: The Golden Sufi Center, 2020, p. 19.

**p. 188:** "**his classic play *No Exit* . . .**": The original play by Jean-Paul Sartre was first published in France in 1944.

**p. 189:** "**Then help us . . .**": From *All the Light We Cannot See,* Anthony Doerr. New York: Scribner, 2014, p. 269.

**p. 190:** "**there is a story or tradition . . .**": I spent thirteen years researching such stories of moments when we have worked well together, across history and different cultures, which culminated in my book on community, *More Together Than Alone.* New York: Atria Books, 2018.

**p. 190:** "**the Kumiai Way . . .**": Details are drawn from Carolyn Kyyhkynen Lee, "A Kumiai Project: Leadership and Social Influence in response to a Community Crisis," PhD diss., University of Southern Mississippi, 2007.

**p. 191:** "**Sometimes it's a form of love . . .**": David Byrne, from an interview, cited as a quote of the day at Best Poems Encyclopedia, https://www.best-poems.net.

### The Mind Is an Inlet

**p. 194:** "**I shall never forget . . .**": D. H. Lawrence, from "New Heaven and Earth" in *The Complete Poems.* New York: Penguin Classics, 1994.

**p. 195:** "**The mind in creation . . .**": Percy Bysshe Shelley, "A Defence of Poetry," in *Criticism: The Major Texts,* edited by W. J. Bates. New York: Harcourt, Brace, Jovanovich, 1970, p. 433. Also cited in full in the chapter "The Unexpected Utterance" in my book *Drinking from the River of Light: The Life of Expression.* Louisville, CO: Sounds True, 2019, p. 11.

### To Look or Not to Look

**p. 197:** "**To Look or Not to Look**": The first five paragraphs appear here as I originally wrote them in *The Book of Awakening* (Newburyport, MA:

Red Wheel/Weise 2000) as the entry "A Great Battle Raging" (March 17, p. 91), in which I first told the tragic but revealing story of Orpheus and Eurydice. It is a theme I have explored for years as my understanding has evolved.

### Here and There

**p. 204: "Here and There":** I have explored this topic for years. My first reflection appeared in *The Book of Awakening* as the entry "Here and There" (July 4, p. 220). My understanding of this has grown and deepened through the many conversations I have had in the many circles I've been blessed to convene.

**p. 207: "There is no here, no there . . .":** Seng Ts'an, from "The Mind of Absolute Trust" in *The Enlightened Heart,* edited by Stephen Mitchell. New York: Harper & Row, 1989, p. 27. Seng Ts'an (c. 606) was an early Chinese Zen master, famous for his instruction beyond duality. Regardless of the question, he would bark at his students, "Not Two! One!"

## BUILDING WHAT CAN SERVE

### Here Abide

**p. 211: "Oh how could Heaven . . .":** T'ao Ch'ien, from "Steady Rain, Drinking Alone" in *The Selected Poems of Tao Ch'ien* translated by David Hinton. Port Townsend, WA: Copper Canyon Press, 1993, p. 62.

**p. 212: "Freedom is only part of the story . . .":** Viktor Frankl, from "If Freedom is to Endure, Liberty Must be Joined with Responsibility" by Caleb Warnock, *Daily Herald* (Provo, UT), May 8, 2005, p. A1.

### Keeper of the Tablets

**p. 220: "Libraries and those who preserve knowledge . . .":** Historical details in this chapter are drawn from a remarkably thorough history of libraries found at Wikipedia, https://en.wikipedia.org/wiki/History_of_libraries

**p. 221: "Chained Library":** The scholar and pioneer in relationship-centered care, Rich Frankel, notes, "Books were so valuable that they were chained in place during the middle ages. Also, books originally had no titles on their spine and were shelved with the text block facing outward."

**p. 223: "The center cannot hold":** This line is from the famous poem "The Second Coming" by William Butler Yeats, written in 1919 in the aftermath of World War I and at the beginning of the Irish War of Independence.

### The Honest Classroom

**p. 224: "Straight are the roads to improvement . . .":** William Blake, *The Portable Blake,* edited by Alfred Kazin. New York: Viking, 1946, p. 255.

### Inside Everything

**p. 237: "What matters . . .":** Arwa Qutbuddin, from her TEDx Bangalore talk, "Unraveling Parental Alienation," December 20, 2019. I was blessed to meet Arwa when she participated in a workshop I taught at The Omega Institute. I encourage you to listen to her talk. You will see that she is a very brave and sensitive soul who has been exiled from her children. Please view her talk at https://www.youtube.com/watch?v=uXuPwo0ZeIM&feature=youtu.be.

### THE HEART IS STILL OUR TEACHER

**p. 239, epigraph: "The space within the heart . . .":** Swami Prabhavananda, from *The Upanishads: Breath of the Eternal,* translated by Swami Prabhavananda and Frederick Manchester. Santa Barbara, CA: Vedanta Press, 1975.

### Toward a Greater Sense of Living

**p. 241: "*The Secret Oral Teaching in Tibetan Buddhist Sects . . .*":** I draw on certain paragraphs here that originally appeared where I first explored this notion, in the chapter "Going Beyond" in my book *The Exquisite Risk.* New York: Harmony Books, 2005, p. 259.

**p. 241: "The most striking of the Tibetan Buddhist doctrines . . .":** From *The Secret Oral Teaching in Tibetan Buddhist Sects,* Alexandra David-Neel and Lama Yongden. San Francisco: City Lights Books, 1967, pp. 74–76.

# PERMISSIONS

Thorough efforts have been made to secure all permissions. Any omissions or corrections will be made in future editions.

Thanks for permission to excerpt the following from other previously published works:

Excerpt from "The Mind of Absolute Trust" by Seng Ts'an, translated by Stephen Mitchell, from *The Enlightened Heart*. Copyright © 1989 by Stephen Mitchell. Reprinted with the permission of Harper-Collins Publishers.

Excerpts from "Unearthed Again," "Fighting the Instrument," and "The Moment of Poetry" from my book *The Way Under the Way,* © 2016 Mark Nepo, with permission of the publisher, Sounds True, Inc.

The poem "Adrift" from my book *Inside the Miracle,* © 2015 Mark Nepo, with permission of the publisher, Sounds True, Inc.

William Stafford, excerpt from "A Ritual to Read to Each Other" from *Ask Me: 100 Essential Poems*. Copyright © 1960, 2014 by William Stafford and the Estate of William Stafford. Reprinted with the permission of The Permissions Company, LLC on behalf of Graywolf Press, Minneapolis, Minnesota, graywolfpress.org.

Flight radar image reprinted with the permission of Flightradar24, Jason Rabinowitz, and Agustin Anaya.

Utagawa Hiroshige (Ando) (Japanese, 1797–1858). *Towboats Along the Yotsugi-dori Canal, No. 33 in One Hundred Famous Views of Edo*, 2nd month of 1857. Woodblock print, Sheet: 14¼ x 9⅛ in. (36.2 x 23.2 cm). Brooklyn Museum, Gift of Anna Ferris, 30.1478.33

# ABOUT THE AUTHOR

© Brian Bankston

With over a million copies sold, **MARK NEPO** has moved and inspired readers and seekers all over the world with his #1 *New York Times* bestseller *The Book of Awakening*. Beloved as a poet, teacher, and storyteller, Mark has been called "one of the finest spiritual guides of our time," "a consummate storyteller," and "an eloquent spiritual teacher." His work is widely accessible and used by many and his books have been translated into more than twenty languages. A bestselling author, he has published twenty-three books and recorded sixteen audio projects. In 2015, he was given a Life-Achievement Award by AgeNation. In 2016, he was named by *Watkins: Mind Body Spirit* as one of the 100 Most Spiritually Influential Living People, and was also chosen as one of OWN's *SuperSoul 100*, a group of inspired leaders using their gifts and voices to elevate humanity. And in 2017 Mark became a regular columnist for *Spirituality & Health* magazine.

Recent work includes *The Book of Soul* (St. Martin's Essentials, 2020), a Nautilus Book Award winner; *Drinking from the River of Light* (Sounds True, 2019), a Nautilus Book Award winner; *More Together Than Alone* (Atria, 2018), cited by *Spirituality & Practice* as one of the Best Spiritual Books of 2018; *Things That Join the Sea and the Sky* (Sounds True, 2017), a Nautilus Book Award winner; *The Way Under the Way: The Place of True Meeting* (Sounds True, 2016), a Nautilus Book Award winner; *The One Life We're Given* (Atria), cited by *Spirituality & Practice* as one of the Best Spiritual Books of 2016; *Inside the Miracle* (Sounds True), selected by *Spirituality & Health* magazine as one of the top ten best books of 2015; *The Endless Practice* (Atria), cited by *Spirituality & Practice* as one of the Best Spiritual Books of 2014; and *Seven Thousand Ways to Listen* (Atria), which won the 2012 Books for a Better Life Award.

Mark was part of Oprah Winfrey's *The Life You Want Tour* in 2014 and has appeared several times with Oprah on her *Super Soul Sunday* program on OWN TV. He has also been interviewed by Robin Roberts on *Good Morning America*. *The Exquisite Risk* was listed by *Spirituality & Practice* as one of the Best Spiritual Books of 2005, calling it "one of the best books we've ever read on what it takes to live an authentic life." Mark devotes his writing and teaching to the journey of inner transformation and the life of relationship. He continues to offer readings, lectures, and retreats.

Please visit Mark online at: marknepo.com, live.marknepo.com, threeintentions.com, and harrywalker.com/speakers/mark-nepo.

*To listen with our heart will change everything, regardless of what we think.*